THINGS WE DON'T TALK ABOUT

SHAKING

THE

TREE

2

BRAZEN. SHORT. MEMOIR.

PUBLISHING

Published by MCM Publishing
2801 B Street, #111
San Diego, CA 92102-2208
www.mcmpublishing.com

A version of *Translating RESPECT* was previously printed in *The Best American Travel Writing 2013*, edited by Elizabeth Gilbert.

Copyedited by Erin Willard
Proofread by All My Best
Book cover and interior design by Monkey C Media, www.monkeyCmedia.com

First Edition
Printed in the United States of America

ISBN (paperback): 978-0-9888882-4-1
ISBN (eBook): 978-0-9888882-1-0
Library of Congress Control Number: 2019953314

For those who have wondered if it was safe or wise to talk about the secrets you carry, this book is for you. For those who hope that sharing the most difficult parts of their story will help others, this book is for you.

May you find solace in knowing you are not alone. We are with you; we are you.

Dear Reader,

Each year we challenge our writing community to dig deep and speak from their hearts, sometimes about what scares them the most. This year, we asked the writers to go deeper than they ever have—to reveal the things that no one talks about.

As memoir teachers, we have long watched a recurring scenario play out in our classes.

Picture this: A writer walks into her memoir class, holding her homework, visibly trembling. When it is her turn to read, she tells the group that she is terrified to expose this part of herself because she has never shared this experience with anyone, and she fears people might view her in a different light. She starts to read, and her voice shakes. She cries just a little bit as she reveals the information that she has feared would cause shame or pain. Then, her voice steadies, and she finishes the last line with a hint of confidence. She puts the writing down, a changed person. She knows what we know. Just having the courage to share her story has already changed her. But the experience is not over.

She looks up to see the entire class is enrapt, often brushing away their own tears. She is quickly surrounded by her fellow writers who share the sentiments that they too had the same experience, or that they were deeply touched by the bravery it took to reveal something so intimate. A closeness ensues. A space of somewhat-holy, common ground has been created. The writer walks out the door, lighter, with more ease, and feeling connected to her community. It may have been the bravest thing she has ever done.

❦

Our goal was to create that experience in a book. We wanted to provide a safe space for writers to share their stories in the hopes that by revealing what we think we cannot, we will realize that we all carry some burden, and that by looking that scary beast in the face—we realize that it doesn't have to hold the power. The power is in the community; the power is in the truth.

We do want to provide a warning that the writers really went there, talking about painful parts of their lives like racism and incest, for example, in sometimes bold and revealing ways. We hope that as you dive into these sacred pages, you see a part of yourself or maybe someone you know. We hope that you too pick up a pen to write down your story, which may illuminate your corner of the world and maybe . . . lighten your soul.

Warmly,
Marni Freedman and Tracy J. Jones

Shaking the Tree, Vol. 2, 2019

brazen. short. memoir.

SECRET BROTHER

ELISE KIM PROSSER, PHD

The shrill ring jolts me awake. It's 5 a.m.

Mom cries, "*Agaya*, baby. Daddy had heart attack! *Chibewah*. Come home."

My heart drops. "Okay, I'll be on the next plane."

On the flight, I'm flooded with childhood memories of Dad: giving me horsey rides, reading me Bible stories, and singing our bedtime hymn: "Father, we thank Thee for the night, and for the pleasant morning light . . ." Back then, I thought my father and the Holy Father were the same.

When I get to the hospital, Mom takes me to intensive care. Dad's unconscious and hooked up to beeping machines. His gray face and inert body make my eyes tear.

I whisper, "*Appa, wassuyoh*." No response. I shake his shoulder. "Daddy, I'm here." I sing in his ear: "Father, we thank Thee . . ." But his paper-thin eyelids remain closed.

The nurse interrupts: "Visiting hours are over." I follow Mom out the door.

"*Mogussuh?*" Have you eaten?

"No, I'm starving." Mom drives us to a café. After we order, she takes a deep breath, then sighs, tapping her heart with her fist.

"*Aigo*. It's finally time to tell you." She looks nervous, in a way I haven't seen before.

"You have a secret brother . . . He was born one year after you."

"What? What are you talking about?" At first, I think it's a joke—or a wrong translation. But her face is dead serious.

"Daddy and I were poor graduate students when I got pregnant. You and your brother were what Americans call 'accidents.' We couldn't afford to keep the second one."

Mom is like a train speeding down a track, like she rehearsed what to say. She sips her coffee then continues matter-of-factly.

"So, we gave your brother to our best friends, the Hahns. Mrs. Hahn had a hysterectomy and couldn't have her own baby. They desperately wanted a son." I feel hot, like she just threw her scalding coffee in my face.

"How—how could you do that?"

"Be quiet! Just listen." My hamburger arrives. But I'm not hungry anymore. After the waitress leaves, Mom continues.

"Reverend Hahn counseled us to give the baby to his brother and wife. In the Bible, Abraham and his barren wife adopted a son. He said, 'You already have a baby daughter. And two older sons in Korea, waiting to come to America. It's God's will.'"

I'm astonished as I try to process this. "Wait. Reverend told you to give *your* baby to *his* brother? Isn't that a conflict of interest?

"Shhh. Don't talk."

I feel like a student in her class being scolded. I bite my tongue. Mom continues her lecture.

"His name is Richard. Daddy studied political science. So, he named him after the first American politician to officially recognize China—Richard Nixon. Daddy believed his name would be forever admired."

My fists are clenched. Angry red crescents from my nails nearly cut my palms. But I don't feel pain; I feel numb.

"The Hahns took Richard to Canada. Professor Hahn got a high-paid teaching job there. If we had kept Richard, we couldn't have finished our PhDs to become professors. Mrs. Hahn had to give up her career."

"Did you keep in touch?"

"The two fathers vowed never to talk about the adoption again. But we mothers secretly exchanged Christmas cards."

Here, I imagine Mom receiving a Christmas card boasting,

Our Richard got a perfect SAT score, was valedictorian, and earned a full scholarship to Harvard! Your Elise wants to be an actress? How cute.

Now I know why Mom insisted I major in business. I picture a two-horse race, jockeyed by our competing Tiger Moms. Mom continues, jolting me back to reality.

"Two Christmas cards ago, Mrs. Hahn wrote that her husband died, and she was sick. Last Christmas card, she wrote that Richard got a new job and moved. Only thirty minutes from here. Don't you see? Reuniting us is God's will!"

I have a lot of questions but feel like I'm in shock. The waitress leaves the check. I look at my untouched burger, the fat congealed. Bile rises in my throat, but I swallow it down.

I pay the bill and follow Mom to the car. We drive home in silence. I feel both incredulous and relieved. This missing piece of my crazy family puzzle is starting to fit into place. Entering the house, as we slip off our shoes, Mom reveals even more:

"Daddy and I met Richard last year. But we kept it secret from you children. Now that Daddy might die, and Richard would come to the funeral, I had to tell you." I choke up hearing 'Daddy might die' and 'funeral.'

"I already arranged for you to meet Richard for lunch tomorrow. Now go to bed."

In the guest room, I weep into my pillow. How could Mom have given away her baby? I am now a mother. I feel desperate to hug my son and never let go. Were Mom and Dad selfish? Or selfless?

I can't sleep. My mind races. Reaching for my phone, I Google "What to do when your Mom says you have a sibling who was given up for adoption." Surprisingly, there's a match! I read,

"There is a ripple effect in adoption on the kept sibling, even if the parents never reveal the secret. The adoptee may wonder all their life about their birth family." I realize our stories are intertwined. Exhausted, I finally fall asleep.

The next morning, I can't decide what to wear. Does this dress say, "Sorry, our parents kept me and gave you away?" In retrospect, I wish I had grown up with a younger brother. Maybe we could've comforted each other when Mom and Dad fought. And when they left. How would our lives have been different if he had stayed with our family?

I'm nervous as I walk to the restaurant. I meet my secret brother for the first time. Over paella. He wears a button-down shirt and wrinkled chinos. He doesn't really look like my two older brothers or me. But we don't look alike, either. Shaking my hand, he says,

"Nuna, I'm Richard."

"My name is Elise." I think: 'Who's Nuna?' Then I realize *I'm* Nuna! Nuna is a Korean term of respect for "older sister." I've never been called Nuna before.

"I'm so happy to finally meet you! I discovered I was adopted twenty years ago. So, I've been waiting a long time, eh?"

"I'm sorry, I just found out last night."

"I had a happy childhood with loving parents. And was lucky to have a stay-at-home mom who cooked my favorite foods after school. We lived in the same home for twenty years. Did you have a happy childhood, too?"

"Sure," I lie. The empty apartment where I lived alone flashes in my mind. Dad, then Mom, returned to Korea to teach. My older brothers didn't want to take care of me. I was only fifteen. Suddenly, I feel jealous of him. *Bro, you dodged a bullet!*

"My adoptive dad was a respected professor in Canada. I guess that's why I became a professor, eh?"

"Really? I'm a professor, too."

"I was recently promoted to full professor."

"Congratulations!" Now I feel competitive. I haven't achieved full professor and probably never will.

"Do you think your mother and father would have wanted to meet me after forty-six years if I weren't a PhD and professor like them?" *No way, Jose. Plumber wouldn't cut it.*

"Yes, of course." I hope it sounds sincere.

"Are you and your brothers close?"

"We only see each other every few years. As my oldest brother says, 'In America, good sibling means you don't cause each other headaches. Or ask to borrow money.'"

After lunch, we promise to introduce our families soon. Back home, I scrutinize our family portrait, taken forty years ago. Dad, Mom, two older brothers, and me. I'm the youngest. Then I imagine a young Richard standing next to me. I didn't know then that I was living with a ghost—a secret brother.

Mom interrupts my reverie.

"We have to go back to the hospital. What did you think of Richard?"

"I like him. We have a lot in common. But why didn't you tell me about the adoption earlier?"

"Koreans don't talk about it." And then she looks at me with a glint of fear in her eyes.

"Don't tell your husband or your son." She purses her lips closed.

As soon as I get home, I tell my husband. A few days later, I tell my son. Years later, I take pen to paper, the only way to express my feelings in a family that stifles the truth.

As I write, I feel disloyal—because Mom wants me to keep the secret. Because Koreans don't talk about it. As I write, I feel empowered—because I'm breaking the chain of secrecy. So, the next generation won't have to carry it. And the more I write, I realize this: I may be Korean, but I'm also American. And Americans talk about it. And write about it. And create art about it.

MOM SHOULD NOT BE TRUSTED

KRISA BRUEMMER

We moved to the island right before I started second grade. I wasn't sure why Dad stayed in Seattle, but I knew how I could find out—eavesdrop when Mom was on the phone.

Mom told her friend, Liz, Dad had been selling coke, but something had gone wrong, and bad guys were after him. According to Dad, someone had stolen the coke. Mom said Dad was full of shit—no one had stolen the coke. Dad and his loser buddies had lost it, right up their goddamn noses. Mom said there'd probably been some skanky little whores too.

Mom told my little brother Josh and I that we'd moved to the island to start over, to have a better life than we had with Dad. Josh was mad that Dad didn't come with us. He was too young to understand.

Mom said I was her very best friend forever. I knew things no one else did, like how Mom had never wanted to marry Dad, how the second Mom graduated high school, she'd moved as far away from him as she could get.

But then Dad got run over by a speedboat and almost died. So, Mom went back home to visit him, and Dad managed to knock her up right there in his hospital bed. Mom said I should be grateful because she tried her best to be happy despite her miserable life, all for me. And I *was* grateful. My little brother Josh was just too young to understand.

Mom always screamed about how Dad had ruined everything, but she screamed a little less when we moved to the island. She was always telling us how exhausted she was, though. Taking care of two little kids in a run-down trailer in the middle of nowhere was a big job.

Although Mom yelled less with Dad gone, she didn't stop. If we asked for something we'd seen on TV, like a Lite Brite, or the newest Barbie doll, Mom would lose it.

"What part of 'WE HAVE NO MONEY' do you ungrateful little shits not understand?" Mom screamed as she ripped the toys we were playing with right out of our hands and threw them across the living room, or into the trash.

Then our car broke down. So, we walked to the store, two miles away. We were trudging back home when an old man offered us a ride. Mom was wary of situations like that, but our trailer was at the top of a steep, winding hill, and the grocery bags were heavy.

The old guy introduced himself as Ray Hall. I thought it was creepy how Ray kept telling Mom how pretty she was. Mom was pretty though, and Ray was really old, so I decided maybe it wasn't such a strange thing to say. Mom went to a party at Ray's house that night and came home with a stack of cash. Mom said Ray was gonna buy all our food stamps.

A year later, Mom didn't have a job, and her new alcoholic loser boyfriend hardly worked. Even though Mom complained about being poor, Josh and I always had clothes our friends wanted—Air Jordans, Guess jeans. Mom said she bought us expensive clothes so we wouldn't be embarrassed at school. Josh said he'd rather have GI Joes, but I loved it when my best friend was jealous of my outfits.

That Father's Day, Mom called Dad. "I've got my own shit to do today. But these kids wanna see you, so your ass better be home."

I worked hard on my Father's Day card, and I was excited. But when we got to Dad's house, he wasn't there. Mom glared at the door, her breath turning into a low, rumbling growl. Josh slipped his arm in front of Mom and pounded on the door.

"He's not here!" Mom grabbed Josh's wrist. "He doesn't care about you, about us. He's a selfish son of a bitch."

Mom stormed off, not looking back until the key was in the ignition. Josh and I dragged our feet, hoping, if we walked slowly enough, Dad's Mustang might come rumbling around the corner.

When we got to the mall, Josh refused to get out of the car until Mom promised him a whole Cinnabon.

I forgot all about Dad once we were inside. Shopping with Mom was like playing dress up with a friend.

Mom got so excited whenever I tried on something she liked. "You have to get those!" she said about a pair of pink jeans. "You'll be the cutest girl in school!"

When I showed Mom the price, she swapped out the tag with something off the clearance rack.

"It's not stealing because they can't prove *we* switched the tags. But never do this yourself."

Mom paid for my pink jeans with cash. Then we went to her favorite store—Nordstrom.

At other stores, we sometimes had to put things back if Mom didn't have enough cash. But we never did that at Nordstrom because Mom was an authorized purchaser on Grandma's Nordstrom account. After Mom had charged three huge bags of clothes, she noticed a seafoam-green sweater. I knew Mom would never wear that color.

"Let's go to Cinnabon," I said as I walked out into the mall.

A moment later, a security guard clasped his hand around Mom's arm and led us to a small, gray room underneath the mall. I squirmed around on an uncomfortable chair, interrupting to insist Mom hadn't meant to take the seafoam-green sweater out of the store. Then a younger mall cop took Josh and me out into a hallway. They told Mom if she entered Nordstrom in the next two years, she'd be prosecuted.

When we left the mall, we drove back to Dad's. But he wasn't home. As I crouched down to see if I could fit our Father's Day cards under the door, Mom ripped them out of my hand and shoved them under the doormat. "I've had enough of your dad's bullshit for one day!"

I could feel tears burning as the torn-off corner of my card fell from my hand. Josh asked if I was okay. I told him it was Dad's fault for not being home.

≹

Years later, when I was home from college for the summer, I caught Mom smoking a joint on the deck. I said it was time to stop sneaking around, smoking weed on opposite ends of the house at the same time. Mom laughed, and soon she was talking about that Father's Day she got kicked out of Nordstrom.

"The look on your face holding that damn Father's Day card, it was too much. I picked up that sweater and walked out."

I inhaled too much smoke and started coughing.

"I think I went a little crazy that day. I thought if I got arrested, your dad would have to come get you, and you could all have your nice Father's Day."

I suddenly felt way too stoned, like there was a rock stuck in my throat. I took a deep breath, hoping the fresh night air might help.

"It wasn't really stealing. It was just a bad plan. When you and Josh left the room that day, I started bawling and 'fessed to the whole thing."

I stared out at the water, avoiding Mom's face. In the decade since that Father's Day, Mom had done far crazier things than stealing. But there was something about that sweater, about that day. I'd been so sure it was an accident. I'd hated those mall cops for stealing our Nordstrom fun. I'd been so angry at Dad for upsetting Mom enough to make that kind of mistake. I wondered how many times I'd been so wrong.

Josh always said Mom's the crazy one. But I'd always blamed her boyfriends, or even myself. Before Mom confessed about that sweater, Josh had come home from a party saying he'd heard Mom's old friend, Ray Hall, was the biggest coke dealer on the island. I said it was probably a rumor. Josh said he couldn't believe someone as smart as me could be so dumb.

For days, what Josh said about Ray had been scratching at me, transforming my memories, and fucking with my head. But until Mom confessed about that stupid sweater, I hadn't let myself admit that Josh was right, that maybe he'd been right all along. I needed a drink of water. I wanted to be by myself. But Mom followed me into the kitchen.

"You're not mad, are you?"

"No," I said, forcing a smile.

The next day, Mom came home with a Nordstrom bag full of "I'm sorry" gifts. She said, "I should've stolen from JC Penney instead. Those were the worst two years of my life when I couldn't go to Nordstrom!"

I wanted to laugh with her, and to keep telling myself that every crazy thing Mom ever did was for the right reasons. But something had changed. I'd been making excuses for Mom since I was a little kid. But I realized, Mom was full of shit. And Mom should not be trusted.

AN INDEX OF SMALL STINGS

HUDA AL-MARASHI

In a lot of ways, I'm an undercover Muslim. The only time I wear a hijab to cover my hair is when I visit the masjid, and my skin is fair, which is common enough among Muslims, who are found in every part of the world.

But people tend to forget that not all Muslims look alike, that we don't walk around announcing ourselves with veils and beards and mustaches.

Because in the average American's eyes, Islam is not a global religion that belongs to over a billion people from all walks of life.

Islam is tribalism. It's austerity. It's fanaticism. It's zealotry.

It's not a suburban mother in jeans and a t-shirt, raised in California, speaking unaccented English, cruising around in a minivan.

And it's precisely because people don't think I am a Muslim that I hear things.

I hear things all the time.

There was the time I was in John F. Kennedy Airport's baggage claim, my firstborn in my lap, and I offered a young woman struggling with the pay phones my cell phone. After calling home, she sat next to me, and we talked about my baby and her siblings.

Then she said, "They say there's going to be a war with Iraq. What do you think"?

My heart sank. I could tell by the tone of her question, the way it leaned with a certain eagerness, how she wanted me to answer. And I didn't want to tell her that my parents were originally from Iraq and watch this moment descend into the kind of exchange that I'd revisit for years, thinking of all the things I should have said.

So, I tried to be vague, general, and I said, "I don't support war of any kind."

"Nobody does," she said, not taking the hint that I did not want to continue this conversation, "but don't you think we need to defend ourselves?"

My heart rate quickened. "No, I don't," I said. "We're not at any risk from Iraq."

"But there's no telling what those people will do," she said.

And with that, we had arrived at the destination I was trying to avoid.

"I am one of those people," I said, wishing I could find more words, better words, words that would set her and everyone like her straight, but right away, she backtracked and stumbled that her father once worked with a Muslim who was a really nice guy.

Then, a few years later, there was my son's first day of preschool. I was sitting in the office, chatting with a Peruvian mother whose son also began school that day. The administrative assistant in the back office called out to the middle-aged woman working at the front desk, "Did you get a load of the father's name?"

My breath suspended. I knew that post 9/11, my husband's once-ordinary Arabic name now had inflammatory connotations.

The front-desk woman quickly got up, perhaps to inform her workmate that I was still there. When she returned, carrying the

14

scent of powdery perfume, she smiled at me awkwardly and asked, "How many languages do you speak?"

"Three," I answered, my voice soft, and in that same nothing voice, I asked, "Was that my husband's name she was referring to?"

"Oh, no," she denied, shaking her head with so much exaggeration her beaded necklaces clacked together.

That afternoon, I walked my son home, my heart racing, but with what? I had no idea how to name this knot in my gut. All I knew was that I felt so unsettled, so sick. Did this woman think she knew something about my husband because of his name? Was an Arabic name all it took to keep this woman from seeing my loving husband, my children's kind and generous father?

Then, several years later, I was at my condo association's yearly garage sale, and a Palestinian woman asked me to give her several household items because she had diabetes, and a sick husband, and a daughter who was married to a terrible man who did not provide for their baby. I imagined she made these requests because we shared the same language, and I told her to take whatever she wanted, and then I helped her load her car where I discovered a trunk full of car seats and baby clothes similar to the ones she picked from my driveway. I pushed away the sense that I'd been hustled with the reminder that the woman was clearly still in need.

Later, at a lull in the garage sale, I walked over to my neighbor and her daughter and asked, "How's it going?"

"Slow," she said, "those Arab women are the worst. They always want something for nothing. But then I think about how awful those women's lives are, and I just want to ask them, 'Do you know Jesus Christ?'"

15

I was certain I'd misheard. It wasn't possible that someone could say something so unbelievably misguided—out loud. I replayed the entire conversation in my head, but before I could open my mouth and object, another neighbor walked by with his dog and stopped to chat; and I didn't know how to steer the conversation back so I could say—excuse me, *What?*

And then, just last summer, there was the time I was writing in a coffee shop, trying to tune out the interview for a sales job taking place at the table in front of me. The employer was grandiose and full of bluster, and he told his applicant,

"Some people are going to say what's a Mexican guy like you doing making five grand a week, but I got no problem with you being Mexican. As long as we speak the same language, I can get along with anyone. I just don't like Arabs. They want to kill my people. They want to kill yours, too. You were here for 9/11, right?"

My fingers stopped moving over the keyboard. I commanded myself to react, to interrupt, to at least make light of his comments in an offhand way, but I was shaking.

I pulled out my notebook, wrote his words down, and pretended this attempt at record-keeping equaled doing something.

Because I didn't know what else to do.

That's the thing about small stings. They catch you off guard while you're just going about your daily business, at the airport, at school, at a garage sale, or in a coffee shop.

This is the kicker with the small stings. You don't even know if it really happened. You were just going about your day when the breath got knocked out of you, and you asked yourself, "Did I hear that right?" And by the time you went over it in your head, it was too late. The moment had passed, and you couldn't go back because you didn't want to be that person, making a big deal out of something that was nothing.

But really, what can I say in those moments? Someone, please tell me how to call out things when I'm completely stunned, and a moment passes so quickly? When people walk away, and subjects change before I've even had a chance to react?

Because each one of these stings is like a brick, stacking up inside of me, their immovable weight reminding me that these are not isolated incidents from one person.

This is how a lot of people feel.

This is what slips out when they think no one of your kind is listening.

DO THEY KNOW?

LAURA L. ENGEL

Where am I? What happened? God, I'm so thirsty.

My eyes are slits, opening to bright white light. That hospital smell, antiseptic along with a bleach-y clean scent, permeates the air. Heavy, stiff sheets feel like lead. The sounds of women's voices register in my ears. I strive to push drugged cobwebs out of my brain. I lick my cracked lips. I try to swallow what seems like wool forced down my throat.

My hand reaches for my baby. Where is my hard hill of a belly? A soft empty sack replaces where my baby lay yesterday. I panic. I don't remember giving birth. My last memory is unbearable pain, a masked doctor, a needle, and nothing.

Where is my baby? Did the baby die? Did I have a boy? A girl?

My mind is blank. My body deflated.

All those months, in my heart, I just knew my baby had to be a boy. I secretly called him Jamie. Now Jamie is gone.

I struggle to push open heavy eyelids and take in my surroundings. I know I'm in a hospital in New Orleans. I know it's July 1967. I know I was admitted yesterday in hard labor. *But what happened after that?*

A small group of women, beds facing each other forming a circle, fill the maternity ward. *Am I dreaming?* No one is paying me any mind. Invisible, I observe them, these laughing women. They chat softly, faces glowing.

Each eagerly tells her story. I longingly watch as they sip from green glasses.

God, I'm so thirsty. They are all older than me. After all, I'm just a teenager. Their chatter goes on relentlessly. As I listen, I realize they are talking about their babies, their deliveries, and their husbands.

I look away. I am not one of these women so confident, so full of laughter. They will keep their newborns. They will go home to their families, their husbands, and they will love and raise their babies. They will know their children forever.

But I am different. I have no wedding ring. My baby is a secret and will not go home with me. Closing my eyes, a hard lump grows in my throat.

"Well, well, our new little mama's awake," the loudest woman in this group of new mothers announces. "You were out, sugar, I mean out!" She has a strong New Orleans accent. She's too loud, too brash. I instinctively know the type. She scares me to death.

What will she ask me? Will she ask if it's a boy or girl? Or, where is my husband?

I begin to panic, but just then, a nurse comes striding into the room. She heads straight to my bed, her hair a fiery red halo. Millions of freckles dot her smiling pink face.

She chortles, "Well, I sure am happy to see you're finally awake! I bet you're hungry as a mama bear."

"Thirsty," I croak.

Without asking, she pulls the stiff sheets from me as she simultaneously whips a curtain around my bed. My face flushes as she peers in between my legs and removes bloody pads from under me, replacing them with clean ones. The metallic smell of blood wafts upward.

All business, she pours me a drink of water.

"You must be starved. I'll get some food up here," she promises with a smile. She's so kind; my eyes tear up.

Her eyebrows rise as she studies a clipboard chart attached to the foot of my bed.

Does it say I'm an unwed mother? Does it say I can't see my baby?

I notice she's still smiling. I relax. It must not state that my baby will be put up for adoption.

Tepid stale water slides down my throat, and I almost cry from the relief. I reach for the pitcher to pour more. Screwing up my courage, I whisper, "Um, ma'am . . . um, my baby? Is my baby . . ."

"Oh, we'll be bringing them out soon."

Bringing "them" out?

As she whips back the privacy curtain and turns to face the women, she loudly announces, "Ladies. Ladies. Feeding time in just a few minutes." Delighted chirping sounds fill the room.

Then turning back to me, she nods her head, "Your baby boy's doing fine. I'll bring him to you. You feel up to feeding him?"

"Oh, yes. Please." My heart swells.

She said my baby "boy" is fine. I just knew it. My boy. My Jamie. My heart soars. *I'm going to hold him. It's too good to be true.*

I lay back and turn toward the wall; my eyes closed. *If they think I'm sleeping, no one will talk to me. No one will ask me questions.*

Another nurse enters the room. " Flowers for Miz Hammond!" The brash woman is delighted. "Oh, my husband, Joseph. He's an angel." I open my eyes and watch as the nurse carries a huge vase of pink hydrangeas across the room. All the new mothers "ooh" and "ahh." There will be no flowers for me.

Minutes later, the cries of newborns fill the room. My eyes open wide and I watch as two nurses enter pushing bassinets, wheels clicking. I pull myself up, sitting straight as I can, my heart pounding so loud I'm sure everyone can hear it.

A petite nurse, blond pixie haircut, walks up to my bed, checks my name on the chart and bends to pick up a tiny bundle, wrapped in gray and blue flannel.

My arms reach out. Wonder fills me to the core.

"Here's your mama."

This is Jamie. This is my baby boy. This is a feeling like I have never felt in my life. This is my heart about to be broken.

I am complete, in awe, as my arms cradle this solid seven-pound boy, wrapped so tightly. Tears wet my face as I intently study the miracle in my arms.

Soft downy cheeks, almond eyes with lashes lying on those cheeks, a tiny perfect rosebud mouth. I softly touch the pale fuzz that crowns his head. *He has my nose. My mouth.* I hold him close; feel the solid weight of him. I breathe his tantalizing new-baby scent.

My son. My heart pounds next to his. Holding him is exquisite joy, exquisite pain.

Tugging at my arm, the nurse says that I'm holding him too tight. She tells me to relax. "Loosen your grip there, mama. He's not going anywhere." She jokes. I flinch.

"Oh, Jamie. It's you." I whisper. "Hey. I'm your mama." Tears fill my eyes. The activity in the room swirls around us, yet we are alone.

Jamie is half awake, his eyes silvery slits, and he could care less about eating. His little face twists into a newborn grimace. His lips latch onto the brown nipple of the bottle, and he sucks. Me, fascinated by this sight; him, mouth working as he sucks, stops, seems to drop off again, sucks, stops, and his eyes open a tiny bit more.

He's perfect. Jamie's mouth goes slack, and he sighs; formula rolls out onto his chin, unquestionably beautiful.

Oh, God, just look at him. I am mesmerized. I am smitten.

I slip my finger in his mouth; he sucks. My chest hurts. Contractions squeeze my insides, hurting, but in a good way. I grasp his tiny hand. His fingers curl around my finger.

His bottle forgotten, Jamie sleeps soundly against my heart. *Please let this be forever.*

Too soon, Pixie Nurse returns. Her brow furrowed, she stomps directly to my bed.

Maybe she sees he hasn't finished the bottle. Her face glares.

She grabs the bottle and reaches for my son.

"Please, no. Let me hold him a little longer, please."

"Times up. He was supposed to stay in the nursery. I'll take him now."

The hostility in her voice startles and embarrasses me. *She knows.* I see it in her eyes. She thinks I'm a monster. A slut. An unfit mother. Not even a mother. Not worthy of holding and feeding my son. I jerk away, Jamie still clasped tight against me.

The red-haired nurse has entered the room and walks directly to my bed. Like a huge, white-flapping stork, she hovers over me. I hold Jamie close and peer up at her. She takes in the scene unfolding before her. Pixie Nurse standing hands on her hips, me clutching my baby to my chest, wet eyes pleading.

The women are all quiet now. Some infant cries out, hushed by a nipple. Silence now as they watch the drama unfolding in our tiny universe. Eager vultures, they wait. I know what they are wondering. "Why are they taking her baby so soon? What did she do?"

The kind red-haired nurse bends close. "Let's not have any problems here, honey."

Before I can protest, Jamie is expertly swooped out of my arms, carried away. As I watch the backs of the nurses leave the room, my world collapses. Cold. Emptiness fills me. *Please, God, my son.*

The women resume feeding their babies, studying their perfect newborns' faces and talking quietly amongst themselves, now determined not to meet my eyes. Not a word is said to me.

I turn away from them; my wet eyes squeezed shut. Humiliated beyond words, shame engulfs me, covering me like a film. My body trembles, holding back sobs. My fists clench.

What did I expect? I am a mother, but am I? A real mother would take her son home. A real mother would not have her child pried from her arms.

The women's grasping eyes burn holes through my soul.

They know.

CRUISING

LAUREN HALSTED

Note to the reader: This true story is based on research and interviews with friends of Fred Halsted, my uncle, who passed away on May 12, 1989.

You're not going to believe how I decided to make my first porno movie. It was a typical day. The summer of 1968. I'm cruising into Echo Park, driving my powder-blue Chevy Impala. The top is down. I can see everything; everyone can see me. Fred Halsted. I'm twenty-six years old. Here from San Jose. Been in L.A. a couple years now. The longest I've lived anywhere.

Growing up with my mom and brother, I never lived in one place longer than a year or two. My mom carted us boys from town to town, looking for free places to stay and enough money to get by. Every time I made a new friend, we'd move. When I was real little, three and four, I'd play with the lizards all day while Mom was at work and my brother was at school. When I found Los Angeles, I stayed. First place I wasn't lonely all the time.

Realizing you're gay in the 1950s was, well, let's just say that if word got out, people were shunned by their families, fired from their jobs, or, sometimes, beat up. So even then the unofficial rule was don't ask, don't tell. When I was a kid, maybe twelve or so, we lived in the back of a hamburger joint that my mom fixed up and opened. Me and my brother served all the food, made milkshakes.

One day, I heard my mom tell two men, "Get out! We don't serve faggots." I never forgot that.

Once I got to LA, I needed to make money. So, I found work as a gardener. One of my gigs is for Vincent Price. Here's this guy, rich and famous. And he's gay. No one knows, but *everyone* knows. But that's Hollywood. Take your wife to the premiere. Then meet the cabana boy in your pool room later. I love the job. It keeps my body hard. Price doesn't seem to mind. More than that, I love getting my hands in the dirt. Planting seeds that grow in ways you'd never expect. All the unique plants making something beautiful.

Now, I'm in my neighborhood—driving down West Sunset Blvd, where I can be myself. At least sometimes. And there's one thing on my mind: finding a guy to ball.

I stop at a red light. I'm looking around. Then my eyes stop. Look at those guys over there. A perfect pair. One's over six feet tall—a real stud. His rock-hard chest pulls his cotton shirt tight. Hair creeps out from his sleeves, around his collar, just like I like. The other's shorter, innocent looking with a cute boyish face. Wearing white shorts and a light-blue cardigan. A twink, my favorite type. I rev my engine to get their attention. I love the naked honesty of it all. Everything out in the open, if you know how to look.

The light turns green. I roll into the intersection. My eyes feast on the pair. One of them, then the other, looks back at me. Their eyes linger. The "scene" has begun.

I pull over and throw the engine in park. The Stud and the Twink walk up. The Stud leans against the passenger door. "Wanna grab a beer?"

The invitation. I kill the engine. My leather boots hit the ground. I slap my palms against my dirty Levi's, releasing puffs of dust into the air.

"Look at this package," the Twink says under his breath.

I hear the comment, like he wants me to. "I know a place right up the block."

"We'll follow you."

The three of us walk in silence toward the bar. It's the kind of place that always smells of stale beer and, once inside, you can't tell the difference between one in the afternoon and one in the morning. The Stud orders beers. I sit at the bar, and the Twink passes close behind me, brushing my back with his hard dick. He continues to the bathroom. The real action's about to begin.

The Twink and I are in this tight, one-toilet room. Not a word passes between us. An unspoken code of safety, fraternity, holds true. I release the top button of my jeans, making some room. The Twink shoves me back again the door. He drops down to his knees. I'm surprised by his forcefulness. "Aggressive for a Twink."

The door opens behind me. I hear the Stud's voice, "I told you not to start without me."

The Stud puts his strong hands on my shoulders. As I hang in anticipation of the soft, wet touch of lips, in more places than one, I suddenly feel cold metal clasps around my wrists.

"You guys are into this? Fuck yeah!" The tight pinch against my skin makes my dick swell even more.

Suddenly, the Stud yanks the cuffs up my back. I stand pinned in position, my hands all the way up to my shoulder blades. And then came the words I did not expect.

"Vice squad. You're under arrest!"

What? Vice squad? Is this a joke?

The Twink in front of me stands up and brushes off his knees. He spits on my boots. My dick goes limp.

I realize it was all a setup—and they're about to drag me outta this bar in handcuffs. I'm sweatin'. Who's gonna see? I retreat into the familiar lie. Don't ask, don't tell.

"Whoa! Whoa! You guys got this all wrong. I wasn't lookin' for nothin'. I just needed to take a piss."

The Stud holds me in a stress position. "Yeah, sure, faggot."

It feels like my elbows are about to break. I bend forward in pain, only to have the Twink kick me back upright. Every impulse tells me to break free from their bondage. But I can't.

The Twink laughs, "That's the beauty of vagrancy. You don't actually have to do anything to be a vagrant. You just are."

My face flushes red. "That charge is bullshit, and you know it. What I did's not a crime."

"On my watch, it is. We are going to get rid of you all one way or another. Permanently." And with that, he drags me off.

Luckily, I have enough money for bail. I go home to John, my lover. He's just as pissed. Not about cruising, of course. I always come home to John. We aren't monogamous. No, John is pissed about the LAPD.

I'm charged with a misdemeanor crime, no real consequences other than a small fine. But I have to enter a plea. Publicly. "Lewd vagrancy" is the catchall charge. The weekend before my arraignment, I spend each night tossing and turning. I can't decide how to plead.

If I plead not guilty, my case will go to trial. It'll be a long, drawn-out process. My word against the cops'. The court's not gonna believe a queer.

The easy solution: plead guilty. I don't talk to my family much. It's not like they'll find out. I'd been arrested for the same thing before, just like almost everyone I knew. We choke down the shame and plead guilty. Just like they want.

It's the Monday morning of my arraignment. The bright sun makes me sick. John and I sit in my car outside the courthouse. "How you gonna plead?" he asks.

"Fuck this." I throw the engine in gear and speed away.

"What are you doing?"

"This is wrong, and everyone knows it."

"They'll put a warrant out for your arrest."

"Let 'em come find me. I'm not playing their games anymore."

In the months that followed, the moment those cops slapped the cuffs on my wrists replayed in my mind, over and over. The anger in their eyes was scorched into my memory. I could no longer hide from it. I needed to confront it. I decided I had something to say about my sexuality. Something beautiful. Something real and honest about who I was and what I did. I'd show the world.

And that's how the decision was made. One night, instead of going cruising, I told John, "I'm going to make a porno movie. A faggot fuck film!"

"What do you know about making movies?"

"Nothing."

Three years later, my first film was projected onto screens across the country. One movie, then two, then twenty. I can still claim that two of my films are the only gay pornographic films in the New York City Museum of Modern Art's collection. The permanent one.

RED SPEEDO

CJ ELLIOTT

He wasn't someone I would have looked at twice. He was older than me, a bit round about the edges. A little effeminate, really, the way he carried his magenta swim trunks down to the beach on a hanger. He was always a dandy, trimming his red-gray beard just so, everything always so nicely pressed. And he talked all the time in a nonstop stream of effervescent ideas that always came back to his favorite subject: himself. My husband and I had known him for years and always thought him a bit of a narcissistic idiot.

But—

After a swim, he invited me to the Pannikin Brockton Villa for coffee. No one had asked me to do anything in years. I mean, I'm a mom. I'm married. My life is a closed system, with internal feedback loops that refer back to my family, my husband, my responsibilities, over and over again.

Coffee? At the Pannikin?

I felt like a girl.

Something within my mind altered as I sat at the café table overlooking the ocean and listened to his voice. Perhaps he said some flattering things. Perhaps he merely asked about the book I was writing—my first. I don't think I talked much. Mostly I remember feeling the flow of his words wash over me like a warm wave. I felt all tumbled about, relaxed. I do remember talking about my husband—invoking his name, perhaps, like an amulet—as I felt something liquid rise in me like xylem awakening in spring. It was strange, heady, considering it was simply coffee between old friends. It wasn't a date, really, was it? He could have been gay, for all I knew; it crossed my mind as he asked where my handsome husband was. My husband was with our child. And there I was, alone in public with another man. I liked it. I wanted to see him again. And when he asked for my email address, I gave it to him.

At home, my husband and I were traveling through a long dark tunnel of despair. We had lost our second child only six weeks before. Our child, sixteen weeks in utero, had, it turned out, a small part missing from chromosome 8, a genetic puzzle piece integral to nearly every organ system. A missing piece. Vital. Fatal. It was left to us to decide if he lived in pain or if he died in peace. Now we had to live with our decision.

We were both grieving in our own ways. My way was to seek comfort—talking with friends and family, visiting familiar places, indulging in small luxuries. My husband's way was to seek isolation, retreating to his art studio or garage. I remember feeling so cold, psychically. Ice cold. I wanted my mother. I wanted the warmth of someone who loved me.

My new Man and I began emailing daily. He'd send poetry and share thoughts and ideas about the world, philosophical ramblings on the nature of art and life. He recommended books to read and movies to see, and I read and saw them all. But it was the subtext of his words, the subtext of his assignments, that grabbed me.

When he told me about the PBS documentary he'd seen on geishas and how they were able to have sex without getting pregnant, was he suggesting we should do that? I felt a frisson of fear. When he told me to watch *Ghost World*, where an older man and younger woman become involved, was he suggesting that, too? When he had me read *Silence of the Lambs* and all the following books, telling me that Hannibal Lecter was his favorite character, was he Hannibal and I Clarisse?

Poetry, conversation, movies, books—everything felt imbued with double entendre. I am enslaved by mysteries. And he was a delicious mystery. And a disturbing one.

He invited me to movies, to swim, to meet at bookstores for readings, for lunch. I invited him to walk with me, made a point to "happen" to be in the places he was likely to be in case I chanced to run into him. Each meeting felt like a bite of forbidden fruit: sour, bitter, tender, and sweet. I was open with my husband as to where I'd be and with whom. But I was not open about how much I wanted to spend time with this man, or how much we were emailing.

My husband was becoming increasingly agitated. One Saturday, I told him I was going to a movie with the Man. While previously he had simply waved me out, this time he stopped and looked me in the eye. "No," he said. "I don't want you to see him anymore."

Reluctantly, I agreed. I agreed because I didn't want a disagreement. I agreed because I didn't want a confrontation. I agreed—but I knew I would not, could not stop seeing him. For the first time in my life, I felt the delicious intrigue of being bad. For the first time, I understood why teenagers want to rebel, why they would lie and deceive. I was the girl who came home before curfew, the mom who never went out with her friends.

I met my Man for coffee and told him we couldn't meet anymore, that my husband didn't want us to see each other. He cocked his head and smiled. "What do you want?" he asked.

I shivered. I couldn't speak. What did I want? What did I really want?

I wanted to—there's no better word for it—sin. I wanted to destroy everything I loved. I wanted to destroy myself. I wanted to blow up everything I knew and loved in a conflagration of illicit self-destructive sex. I wanted to prove to the world I was the monster I knew I was inside, the terrible mother who had let her baby go.

I also wanted to love and be loved. I wanted a husband who held me in his heart. I wanted forgiveness for the death of my son. I wanted my toddler to grow up with two parents who loved him and who loved each other. I wanted to be healed.

Around this time, I read a newspaper article entitled "The Birds and the Bees," about emotional adultery. The article described exactly what I was doing. I was straying from my marriage, even though I had never touched this man. The article described the stages of an emotional affair: casual talking, intimate talking, intimate talking about the problems in one person's marriage, emotional connectedness, casual touching, intimate touching, full-blown affair. Emotional affairs are as damaging as physical ones, the article said. And I knew it was true. While I had not spoken of my marriage and troubles, it was only a matter of time.

I did the only thing I knew how to do: I prayed. I prayed as if my life depended on it. At the same time that I was looking for opportunities to meet my mystery man, I prayed for deliverance from the addictive feelings of lust and infatuation.

One morning I got an email from him that sent shivers of pleasure and fear and alarm through me. "I dreamed about you last night . . ."

I made plans to meet him again, at a public pool for a lap swim, my hand shaking as I hit "send" on the email. Could I tell him I wouldn't see him again? I didn't think I could bear another loss—the end of mystery, possibility, wonder, the depth of grief.

When I got to the pool, I sat on the bleachers in my racing suit, my breathing shallow, bathing cap and goggles dangling idly. I listened to families chatter, watched swimmers stretch, watching the locker room door, waiting. When he emerged, I gasped.

The afternoon sun spilled over the pool deck, bathing eucalyptus tree trunks in golden light, illuminating everything—including my mystery man. There he was, a vision of wonder, clad in a skimpy red Speedo, his middle-aged paunch glowing over his suit like Santa's luminescent belly.

In an instant, everything I had felt for so many months vanished completely, drained from my body like air whizzing out of a balloon. My infatuation was completely gone. I was free, free at last. Thanking God's sense of humor, I was free at last.

TRANSLATING RESPECT

LENORE GREINER

"Signorina, per piacere?"

I looked up into the ebony face of David, an earnest young Nigerian man, perhaps twenty years old, both of us students at the University of Foreigners in Perugia, Italy. In his clipped Italian, David had just haltingly asked me to translate an American song for him and his fellow Nigerian students. The group, expectant and sincere, watched from across our dorm's dayroom.

In our school's Italian immersion program, our international student body consisted of South Americans and Japanese, Danes and Iranians, Americans and Nigerians. Outside our school's palazzo, the Perugini townspeople impatiently put up with most of our slow, sometimes nonsensical Italian. But it was different for the Nigerian students. They seemed to be instantly despised.

"Whenever there's a drug case in the newspaper, it's always the Nigerians. The Nigerians!" spat one storekeeper. This wasn't true; plenty of Americans ended up as guests in Italian prisons as well.

I had seen groups of Nigerian students, Othellos in well-cut Italian overcoats, crossing the Piazza Quattro Novembre, the public drawing room of this Umbrian hill town. I had wondered how they wound up here. I learned later that Italy was exploiting the gas fields of the Niger Delta and needed translators. I wondered how they felt, walking these streets, as they endured the looks of disdain.

David turned up the volume on his battered cassette player, and I took in the unmistakable earthy notes of Aretha Franklin's timeless song, "Respect." I couldn't help but smile as I nodded and said, "*Certo.*" I realized how odd it felt to smile. I was alone in Italy for a year of school, away from home for the first time. The Italian city was bone-chilling cold in a way I had never experienced, and I was deeply homesick. Worse, I felt lost in a pool of unprocessed grief; during my first month in Perugia, an older Turkish student had raped me.

I told no one.

My journal entries stopped on November 7 and didn't start again until December 1, a lost month. I beat myself up, wondered how I had let it happen.

I soldiered on. I made myself numb. I woke up every morning and got myself to class. At night, I escaped my poorly heated pension room to medicate with alcohol and cigarettes in a womb-like cavern of a club, dancing till all hours. With hot water only two days a week and not enough heat to warm the room, combined with my depression and lack of sleep, I found myself terribly sick with bronchitis. I searched for new lodgings and met the nun that ran the dorm for the international students. When she mentioned that they not only had central heat but hot water on a daily basis, I practically kissed her and moved in two hours later.

The dorm, run solely by nuns, was constructed with heavy fortified doors that both secured and separated the men's and women's areas. Save for this one common room, there wasn't much opportunity for men and women to mingle. And now, as Aretha belted out her anthem of the feminist movement that oozed with sexuality, I was crossing the stone-tiled floor in the common room to translate "Respect" into Italian for Nigerians.

It felt so delightfully wrong.

Right at the top of the song, I hit a wall.

Aretha is singing about what he wants, and what's she's got.

David looked confused. "What does she have that I want?" he asked.

How to translate Aretha's innuendo? How to translate a molten, sexual African American soul song in a windowless dayroom in a nuns' dormitory? To Nigerians?

"Well, she has what you want … "

"Yes?" Those earnest faces.

"But all she needs from you is respect." I realized it sounded chaste in Italian.

"*Rispetto.*"

As the Nigerian students leaned toward me, I began scribbling each heated lyric in English, singing along as David stopped and rewound the tape. They grinned and laughed as I sang, crowding their knees toward me as we sat on the stiff furniture. The dictionaries came out: English and Italian, Nigerian and Italian.

I leaned back, feeling relaxed for the first time in months. I realized that it was the first time I felt comfortable and safe around men. My adventurous Italian year had gone so horribly sideways, yet here I was, delighting in a little bit of home, in a little bit of raw sexuality.

Aretha sang about giving everything, and leaving the attitude at the door. This sister was taking control, demanding from her future lover the respect she deserves.

Trading glances, their expressions slowly changed, some forming sly grins as others averted their eyes in shy embarrassment.

They got it.

Aretha continued to drive it home as her backup singers were singing what sounded like sock it to me.

"Ah ... *un po' di piu*," I said, frustrated. The little bit part was coming off as much too dainty; I was not conquering the Italian divide as I wished. I continued.

Ah, yes, how to explain TCB? Where did it come from? During the '60s, on the streets of black neighborhoods, TCB meant "takin' care of business." Later, Elvis brought TCB to white America. Did Aretha want to get this respect question settled pronto so that other "business" could get taken care of?

I looked at my watch. Our dorm's curfew fast approached as Aretha swooned about her lover's kisses, sweet like honey but, hey, so is her money. At this, the Nigerians roared and slapped each other, bending over with laughter. Oh, yeah, Aretha was sassy.

In spite of all the dictionaries, hand movements, and my translation efforts, I wondered, could I truly do justice to Aretha? But did it matter? Here, with my new friends, I couldn't remember laughing so hard.

Finally, my Waterloo: that 60s catchphrase of "Sock it to me."

"Like hit?" asked David. "She wants to be hit."

"No, no, American ... " I raced through the dictionary for the right word. "*Gergo*, slang."

Now long brown fingers spun the pages of the Nigerian dictionary.

"It's like, it's like she wants him to love her, right now," I said, avoiding the temptation to do any pantomiming.

"American slang," said David. "Okay." They got that, too.

As the minutes ticked away and curfew loomed, David rewound the tape, and we all stood up and sang the entire song together, shouting out each letter of the word respect. And at that moment, it hit me. I was a white girl teaching Africans a history lesson on the African American experience during my country's time of great upheaval as women and blacks battled intense sexism and racism.

And I also knew that in this provincial Italian town, these Africans might have been experiencing racism for the first time, insidious and unsaid.

In our camaraderie, as our curfew arrived, we all sang along at the top of our voices together.

And for a few powerful moments, we overcame our collective loneliness.

As the song concluded, as the last healing words washed over me, I realized that Aretha wasn't the only woman who would be demanding respect. Going forward, Aretha's song would need to be mine.

THE PROMISE

DONNA L. JOSE

2007. I didn't remember my promise until the investigator arrived, talking autopsy. After the paramedics and the firefighters had left. After the deputies had gone back to town. After the medical examiner's ghouls had removed my husband's body from the house to an unmarked white van. Until then, I'd been struggling to wake up.

The sheriff and I stood next to the rose bed, just past the porch. The crimson blossoms were in full bloom and sweetly fragrant, but I looked past them at the front door and closed my eyes.

Maybe when I opened them, my husband, Kim, would be there, standing in the doorway. Long silver hair trailing down his back. His mouth turned up at the corners in a playful smile. "I was out back, Donna," he'd say. "I haven't gone anywhere, babe." But when I opened my eyes again, he wasn't there.

"Is this really happening? Am I awake?" I asked the sheriff and swallowed hard.

The sheriff didn't hesitate.

"Yes. You're awake. It's real," he said. "I'm sorry. Do you understand what I'm saying?"

I nodded because I couldn't speak.

We watched as the paramedics emerged from the house with the equipment they used to turn my living room into a mini-ER. I'd been with them while they worked on Kim—until the fire captain made me leave. Kim's body had been on the living room floor, an oxygen mask affixed to his face, his hair splayed out around his head like a silver fan. I had rubbed his legs up and down and called to him to come back. I knew he'd heard me because the heart monitor blipped. It was flat, and then it blipped. Even the paramedics thought they had him for a few brief seconds.

"I'm going to check on my daughter at the neighbor's," I told the sheriff.

"Someone from the medical examiner's office will be here soon," he said.

When I returned home, a tall, thin woman wearing a navy-blue suit, matching pumps, and a dour expression stood waiting for me in my living room along with the sheriff. My husband's body was gone. She seemed young, too young for this job, anyway.

"State law requires an autopsy be performed," she said, matter of fact.

"He wouldn't want an autopsy. I don't want an autopsy. He died of a heart attack."

"Your husband died at home. It's mandatory," she insisted.

"I don't want his body cut up, disfigured."

We went back and forth for several minutes. Well-practiced, she never deviated from her script.

The sheriff spelled it out to me as he stood at my side. "An autopsy will clear you of suspicion," he said in a low voice.

"You can write the medical examiner a letter, make your request, but I can't guarantee anything," she said.

Watching me search the table behind me for a pen and paper, she softened for a moment.

"There are actually different kinds of autopsies. Some are non-invasive." She excused herself and went outside to wait. Three failed drafts later, the sheriff dictated the words to me in whispers. I don't remember his words, but wanted to write this:

I respectfully request that you not mutilate my husband's body because I won't be able to keep my promise to him—the promise I swore I'd keep.

❧

Twenty-three years earlier. I heard Kim at the front door of our apartment, and a couple of seconds later, he'd let himself in and stepped into the kitchen where I was washing dishes.

He'd been working in the garage and had wrapped a turquoise bandanna around his head that made him look like an Egyptian pharaoh. His long dark hair snaked down his back in a low ponytail. He was unshaven and gritty dirty with a sweet sweat smell.

Moving behind me, he wrapped his arms around my waist and brushed his face against my neck. We stood like this for a minute, my hands still submerged in the soapy dishwater.

"You're sending chills down my back," I said and flexed my neck.

His arms tightened around me. "I need to talk to you about something," he said in my ear. Then he kissed my hair lightly and stepped back where I could see him. I couldn't read his expression, but there was a certain earnestness in his voice.

I rinsed and dried my hands on a dish towel and, facing him, readied myself for what was coming.

"Donna," he said, his voice catching on my name. When he faltered the second time, he looked down at his hands clasped over mine, then back at me.

"You're scaring me," I said and gave his hands a little squeeze.

"Do you remember what Billie told me?" Billie was a psychic from the Spiritualist church where we'd met.

"Billie said that I was *the one* and you'd be a fool not to see that?"

He laughed weakly at my joke before his face turned serious again. "Do you remember what she said?"

I rested my forehead on his chest and closed my eyes.

"That you'll die young?" I said into his chest. "You know I wish she had never told you that."

I buried my face deeper. Kim slid his hand under my chin and lifted it, so I had to look at him.

"Hey, is she supposed to say stuff like that? Tell people when they're going to die? Isn't that against the psychic code or something?" I asked.

"It's okay that she told me. I wanted to know."

His voice was gentle, meant to soothe me, but I squirmed in his arms.

"What does this have to do with anything anyway? Why are we talking about this?"

"I want you to promise me something," Kim said.

"Promise what?"

I pulled just far enough away to see his face, the emotion dancing in his eyes.

"Promise me that when it happens, when I die, that you'll wait three days before doing anything with my body."

I swallowed a sigh.

"It all fits. Who I am. Who you are," he said.

We were in the habit of reading spiritual texts and books on metaphysics to one another. A favorite of his was a book on reincarnation which outlined the multiple lives of historical and legendary figures. According to the book, Pharaoh Akhenaten was Jesus was Buddha was Merlin was George Washington was Abraham Lincoln. But, in our conversations about past and future lives, about destiny and fate and purpose and mission, he'd never said what he truly believed about his own destiny so directly or concretely. He'd never said, "I am Jesus Christ come back." But now, he was asking me to wait three days if he died. Three days? Jesus died and rose on the third day, on Easter.

"You're going to die and come back. Resurrection."

"Promise me?"

I watched as waves of disparate emotions crossed his face: hope, fear, anxiety.

"Yes, I promise," I said at last.

I saw the glint of relief in his eyes, but silently I begged him not to leave me.

꙰

Before I met Kim, there was a piece of me missing. Emptiness was taking over. I had convinced myself that I'd never find love. Nonetheless, I sat in the dark, lit a pink candle, and asked the universe for help. Just like the psychic told me to do.

"Please bring me my perfect match," I'd said. And then, poof, there was Kim. Gorgeous, charismatic, funny, kind, and smart. Better than my prayers. For the first time, the hardwiring that told me I wasn't worthy got overridden, and I let myself fall in love. I was Nefertiti to his Akhenaten, the Lady of the Lake to his Merlin.

Driven by love, I suspended my disbelief. I was too afraid of losing him to do otherwise. And even when, much later, it became undeniable that he had propelled himself into madness, I wondered about my part in his breakdown, about what was truly real and what was not.

2007. I knew that the woman from the medical examiner's office had lied to me as soon as I saw the thick plastic bag the medical examiner had returned Kim's body in. It was zipped all the way to his chin. I knew this for sure when the funeral director tried to divert my attention away from opening the bag.

"Someone at the morgue brushed his hair," he said and motioned toward Kim's head.

It was enough to distract me from unzipping the bag. I kissed his forehead, stroked his hair, and asked for a strand.

There would be no coming back in this body.

⁂

Soon after Kim's death, I devised my own version of resurrection for him. A do-over. He'd quietly return to me for a sweet second chance at the life we'd promised each other. I thought it possible for the longest time.

When it seemed to me that he was taking too long, I raged against him like a madwoman—even in my dreams. Instead of embracing him in the dreamscape, I screamed at him night after night for leaving me. He just stood there calmly, never saying a word.

In life, signs abounded. He'd whoosh past me in a crowd, whisper my name in the silent dark, and press his body against me in that trippy time between sleep and wakefulness.

"Let go," he seemed to say.

Against the weight of time, my delusions gave way. I accepted his death and moved forward. But, in the secret places of my heart, I still wonder about what is truly real and what is not.

MACH ZERO

JAMES ROBERTS

It's April 2014, and I'm recently homeless and miserably drunk. After thirty years of dulling the naval-career stress with alcohol, the bill has come due.

If you drink hard enough, for long enough, bad things happen; and after one too many relapses and countless broken promises, my family is fed up. My wife has just asked me to move out, and the look of sadness and confusion on my ten-year-old son's face as I walk out the door almost buckles my knees.

It's a vicious cycle: my anxiety is so overwhelming that alcohol offers the only relief. But after each brief drunken respite, the anxiety bounces back. Stronger. The confluence of panic and depression focuses my thoughts on a question: Glacier Point or Taft Point?

I weigh which spot has the best features. Both are over 7,000 feet in elevation, with stunning views of Yosemite Valley. But for this particular decision, the view is irrelevant. I'm thinking of killing myself—jumping to a conclusion, so to speak. Glacier Point is easiest to get to. I can almost drive right up to the overlook. But it's one of the most crowded places in Yosemite, and I'm not looking for an audience.

I shift my thoughts to Taft Point. Its relative isolation and sheer drop make it ideal, with one step separating the 7,500-foot cliff from the 4,000-foot valley floor. It requires a short one-mile hike, but I'd been on that trail at least ten times before. I could do it drunk or sober. The only speed bump was whether Glacier Point Road would be open this early in the season. Siri informs me indifferently that the road is open. Siri doesn't care about my motive.

I throw a tent and sleeping bag in the trunk of my car and head north. The uselessness of bringing camping gear on a suicide trip does not cross my mind. I've always fantasized about running away to Yosemite; it's my favorite place on the planet. But now it has a more ominous draw—a chance to forget the crushing guilt of failing as a husband and father. I imagine standing at the edge of Taft Point and free-falling to the valley floor, a last flight for a former navy pilot.

In a twisted way, the thoughts of suicide are calming; a mantra to convince myself there is a way out of the misery. When things get this bad, it helps to imagine you still have some control over your life, even if that control is how to end it. This is what addiction has done to me—made the irrational seem reasonable, the stupid sound sensible.

Heading north on I-5, I cross into Orange County, my home until I left for the U.S. Naval Academy at seventeen. A freeway billboard for Disneyland manages to break through the white noise of intoxication. I'm sober enough to appreciate the irony of passing "The Happiest Place on Earth" while contemplating suicide, and with that lucidity, I realize that perhaps things are moving too fast. Maybe I should stop and think this through.

I pull off on the exit to Disneyland and park on a side street near my old house. I grew up two blocks from the park, and the area triggers a montage of memories. There is a boutique hotel where my elementary school stood. My junior high is now the Disneyland parking structure. Across the street used to be an orange grove—and our de facto park, where we played a primitive version of paintball using rotten oranges as ammunition. As I recall the pungent smell of the oranges, I'm taken back to a time before alcohol ...

On summer nights, just before nine o'clock, the kids on our block would gather on front lawns, waiting for a neighborhood tradition: the Disneyland fireworks. They were a multi-sensory display of brilliant colors, chest-thumping booms, and, if the wind was blowing right, the smell of sulfur and whatever other periodic elements they put in fireworks back then. When the grand finale's last echo died off, it meant our day was over. The influence of the Magic Kingdom even extended to our bedtime.

Disneyland of the 1960s lacked the massive infrastructure of hotels, restaurants, and shops that surround today's theme parks. It was embedded right in the middle of our middle-class neighborhood. The iconic Sleeping Beauty's Castle was visible from my kindergarten classroom. And while our school playground wasn't literally in the shadow of the Matterhorn, the screams from the rollercoaster mixed with the screams of students at recess—and that was just normal.

For a kid, it's hard to overstate the coolness of living next door to Disneyland. For just sixty cents (ages twelve and under), my friends and I could enter a fantasy world without adult supervision. On summer days, if we could scrape together the cost of admission, we would head east two blocks, past our school, across the massive parking lot, and step inside Walt's wardrobe.

Sitting in my car, I roll up the windows—muting the fireworks but not the memories. On autopilot, I continue driving north. I feel I have nowhere to go and nothing to live for. Most of my family still lives in Orange County, and as I approach the exit for my sister's house in Anaheim Hills, the urge to talk to someone suddenly overwhelms any other. Maybe in the back of mind, that was my destination all along.

My text that I am in her driveway brings a quick reply: "Stay there, I'll be right home." As my story pours out, she provides the empathetic ear I need. As a mom, my sister instinctively knows to play the strongest card in her hand—my children. She talks about the repercussions of them growing up without a father, and I feel something shift inside me. Handing her my keys, I feel both the relief of choosing life and the uncertainty of a missed opportunity to end the misery.

Of course, it is the right choice. But even the right choice has consequences. At that moment, surrendering alcohol feels like an existential loss. I am afraid of losing the freedom of self-medication. But what freedom did I really have in addiction? Alcohol was in the driver's seat.

Two days later, a couple of navy pilot friends transport me to my first rehab at the VA Hospital in La Jolla. They used to work for me, now they're all grown up and commanding squadrons. I think of the times I rescued them from alcohol-related incidents as junior officers, and laugh in spite of myself at this "circle of life" moment.

Growing up in an environment where fantasy and real-life lived so comfortably next to each other was unique. When addiction had me by the throat, I was looking for something other than myself to blame. In rehab, I listened to the horrific childhood stories of other addicts and alcoholics and thought back on my own sublime life as a kid. I was left with nothing to explain my predicament. No abuse, no tragedy. No dislocation, bullying, or divorce. Maybe that left me unprepared for the ignorance, stress, and injustice of the adult world.

Is the explanation for my addiction that simple? Hardly. Besides, the "Why me?" part of addiction isn't half as important as the "What now?" part. For me, writing is one piece of the solution. It helps heal the shame of this thing I don't talk about. And, although I can never call myself *cured*, I do have moments where I'm overwhelmed by this second chance I've been given.

Just two years later, my wife and twelve-year-old son and I are on our way to Yosemite together. As we pass the tallest trees on earth, I think back on the moment my navy pilot friends walked me into rehab. Then, with the help of the counselors, I stared down my anxiety, taking it apart piece by terrifying piece.

The three of us climb up to Taft Point together. Hands offering help, pulling one another up, slowly, gently, protecting life.

Sober, my feet and mind are planted firmly on the granite cliff's edge.

We breathe in the view. Then turn to make our way home.

GOING DEEP

BILL PETERS

When my head hit the bottom of Midge Lake that night in the summer of 1971, my first thought was about the sand in my hair. But I discovered I had bigger problems. Like, why couldn't I stand up, and where did everyone go? My arms flailed in the water as I tried to stay afloat, but my legs were dead weight. A gasp for air brought only water. My call for help was barely a gurgle. Dark water covered me.

By the time my body was found floating in the lake, it was so rigid that a stick had to be used to pry open my jaw for artificial respiration. An ambulance was called, but got lost, so someone had run out to the highway to wave it down with a white T-shirt. I remember a moment of clarity in the ambulance as the sirens screamed down the road. My eyes opened, and I saw a nurse's face lit up by the lights from the dashboard. She put a hand on my forehead.

"Stay with us, Bill," she whispered. I was twenty-two years old.

I woke again in a brightly lit hospital room, crisscrossed with tubes and wires. My only view was of the ceiling tiles bursting with tiny black dots. Hissing sounds. A nurse was moving about the room. When I saw Mom and Dad standing at the foot of my bed, I knew it was serious. So, this is where the party ended. The nurse left the room, and a doctor entered. He eased himself over to my bedside, and his eyes came to rest on mine. He spoke softly.

"Bill, we have a couple issues regarding your situation. We have been fighting to keep air in your lungs and get the water out. This will take time, but I think we will be successful. The other issue ... " He paused, and I listened with ferocious attention.

"Let me ask, did you dive into the lake?" I nodded, yes. "Well, you may have damaged your spinal cord, which is why you are unable to move your legs." I closed my eyes and tried to move my foot, but I couldn't even tell if I had a foot. "I am going to recommend that we transfer you to Saint Luke's Hospital. They have the necessary equipment and staff for the recovery process."

Recovery? I didn't trust that word. I thought spinal cords broke forever.

The doctor turned to my parents, and they all walked out to the hallway. In the silence of the room, my mind screamed to my body, "What have I done to you this time?" I'd brought enough drama to my family, acting on whims, wandering about the country, hitchhiking through Europe, sampling drugs, and taking life for granted. Now what?

Alone in the room, I tried to scrape the sand out of my hair, but my fingers were too feeble. I clenched my teeth in itching agony. When the nurse came back, she asked if I needed anything. It took me three breaths to answer.

"Can you ... get the sand ... out of my hair?"

"I will surely try," she said. Pulling up a chair, she began slowly running a comb through my hair. With each stroke, grains of sand fell into a metal bin with a hollow ping. Again, and again. I closed my eyes and began to relax. For a moment, the wind was in my face, my body was floating behind me, and my fingers were holding the handlebars of a bicycle as I drifted downhill.

The previous Friday started out with good intentions. When I graduated from college two months earlier, my student deferment to the military officially expired, so I figured it was time to serve my country. I'd made an appointment with a recruiting officer to ask if I could work in a hospital or a senior center instead of shooting strangers in Vietnam, but nothing was promised.

Our conversation left me in a dark mood. I walked the streets of our small town with my hands in my pockets until Art came by in his Chevy. Together, we drove around town listening to the Minnesota Twins on the radio. The team was doing lousy, but Harmon Killebrew was hitting home runs. In his career, he had hit 499 of them, to be exact. Everyone was waiting for number 500.

At a stoplight, a girl in a Volkswagen told us about a party on Midge Lake, so we followed her ten miles down the Old Cass Lake road, and another mile down a dirt road. Laughter and Led Zeppelin poured out the windows—an unofficial invitation for anyone. Before going inside, Art and I paused at the bonfire and met a few neighbors, then we wandered down to the lake and looked out at the stillness. Such contrast: the turmoil of the party behind us, the reflection of distant lights sparkling on the water in front of us. We kept walking along the shoreline until we could hear only the call of distant loons.

Back inside, a call went out for poker players, so I sat down, drank a few beers, and won a few dollars—aces backed with sevens. At midnight, a band of revelers stripped off their T-shirts and ran to the lake. We used a raft anchored offshore as a diving platform. By the time I joined the group, I was last in line. As they scurried back to the cabin, I was in midair, waiting for the big splash.

On Monday, a tracheotomy was cut into my throat to create a hole for a breathing tube. Two more holes were drilled into my skull so that rods could be inserted. These were attached to cables that were strung through pulleys, allowing ten-pound weights to hang near the floor. This separated my vertebrae so they could heal properly.

"These rods will be removed once the bones have healed," Dr. Andrews told me.

"Okay, I got time," I told him with defiance. "Let's get on with this process. I got things to do, and I can't do them lying here."

On Tuesday, Dad brought a transistor radio so I could listen to the baseball games. Reception was fuzzy in the ICU, but now I tuned in every night. *Waiting for number 500. Waiting to walk again.*

There were awkward moments. Like when a nurse placed a box of Kleenex on my chest so I could wipe my nose. I didn't have the strength in my hand to pull one tissue from the box.

There were days of disbelief. Like on my sister's first visit when they pulled the curtain away from my bed. Our eyes met, and she crumpled to the floor. She explained later that she hadn't eaten any breakfast and was a little lightheaded.

There was high anxiety. Like the first night, they let me sleep on my own without a respirator breathing for me. Air whistled slowly in and out of the tracheotomy hole. Then suddenly, I was underwater again, and the surface was out of reach. I could not get enough air, and I could not find the call button. I started clawing at the ceiling and rattling my side rails. Nurses heard the noise and came running. They rescued me, but I collapsed into deep despair, wondering if this would be the new normal for falling asleep.

There were moments of surprising gratitude. Like when I woke up to the sound of sirens wailing and a girl's screams. More frantic wailing in the hallway, and finally in the ICU itself. She had a traumatic head injury from a motorcycle accident. The moaning rose and fell the rest of the night and into the next day. I lay silently on a gurney, dead from the chest down with two spikes in my head, unable to breathe on my own, and felt blessed.

There were moments of hope. Like when Mom came in and took my hand. "Be careful," she'd said a million times. Now her eyes were filled with sorrow. She'd always let me run wild in the grassy fields of life. My eyes spoke to her, taking full blame for the predicament I was in. I was no war hero; I was just stupid—diving half-drunk into unfamiliar waters at midnight. But we didn't talk about that. Deeper in our gaze, I also saw a glimmer of hope, as if we each held a piece to some secret puzzle that we might solve together.

There were moments of glorious, simple pleasure. Like when Dr. Andrews said that day-by-day, I could try more solid foods, which my brother interpreted to mean that what I really needed was a bucket of Kentucky Fried Chicken. I could smell it coming down the hall. Using two napkins and two wrists and no fingers, I got three good bites of a drumstick. We tuned in the Twins game and learned that Mister Home Run King hadn't hit one in six days. He went down swinging in the first inning. As the game droned on, the drumstick settled in my stomach like a Thanksgiving dinner.

There were moments when I lied to myself in my dreams. Like when I closed my eyes and eventually dozed off. In my dream, I suddenly lost my fear and became inexplicably optimistic. I would be the exception. My spinal cord would heal. One year, two maybe. Health care was so much better. It was the Space Age. Miracles happen. Killebrew might even hit that home run we were waiting for, and I might be dancing this time next year.

GLASS SHARDS

NANCY "PANTS" JOHNSON

Mutton chops. I couldn't take my eyes off them. It didn't matter
that my summer bio teacher, Mr. Engberg, lectured about habitats. I
was sixteen and only focused on the tall, muscular teacher's assistant
with the alluring blue eyes and sandy-brown muttonchops.

After several weeks of eyeing each other and pretending we
weren't, I sensed Mark approach the desk where I stood dissecting
a frog.

"Hey. I'm wondering if you'll go to a movie with me
tomorrow night."

Mark acted like a perfect gentleman. He didn't even try to kiss
me. While we snuggled at the drive-in, I stroked his thick, curly
sideburns, and he held my hand in his big, masculine senior hand. I
loved his kind, sexy, and shy grin.

In September, after two months of dating, Mark picked me up
every day in his blue Chevy, and we necked in the car before school
started. He walked me to my classes, kissed me goodbye, and picked
me up at the end of class. The first time I went to Mark's house, his
parents and two younger brothers had just completed a puzzle of a
nude centerfold. Mark looked uncomfortable, while his family made
crude comments about the woman's body parts. My inculpable
Mark, on the other hand, strove to be born again, and together we
attended a fundamentalist youth group. The poor guy, trapped in
a demented household with deranged parents, aspired to listen to

the angels as they circled like a halo around his head. We completed homework together, and Mark landed a job at Farrell's Ice Cream Parlour. We struggled to contain our kissing and touching and debated over just how far God would want us to go.

Soon after Mark graduated from high school, and we had been dating one year, he decided he wanted to move into an apartment with a friend. When he told his mom, Ruby, about his plans, she kicked him out in a rage. Her impaired plan was to shock Mark with her threat to throw him out so that Mark would confess his sins and go back to obeying his mother's every command. But her outburst brought about the opposite effect. Mark spent a few nights at a friend's house, and after one or two heated phone conversations, asked his parents if he could come by for his things.

Up to this point, I had heard about, but never witnessed, a Mom hurricane. Mark wanted me along because he thought his mom wasn't as likely to be volatile if I was present. He rang the bell. How bizarre it must have been to already feel like a stranger in his own home. Mark held tight to my hand and when the door opened, we were both jerked inside. The door slammed behind us, and the first thing I heard was the clack of the bolt turning in the lock. It took a few minutes for my eyes to adjust to the darkness of the musty, smoky room. Mark's mom, Ruby, had a glass of wine in one hand and a cigarette in her mouth, as she methodically circled the room. She locked every window and pulled every shade. She was a large, wide-shouldered woman whose hips were held up by scarecrow legs. Her sizeable breasts heaved in and out far more than necessary to maintain normal breathing. Her mouth imitated a dried-up prune, with a circle in the middle large enough to insert the cigarette that was the source of the smoke screen.

My organs tightened and twisted within my body. One small place in the corner shade was torn. It left a triangular-shaped stream of light that peered into the dreary room. Smoke from two hours' worth of chain-smoking raced to the stream of light.

As my eyes adjusted to the room, I saw what must have been *all* of Mark's belongings strewn across the living room floor. The broken spokes and bent seat of his new ten-speed bike told the story of someone in a frenzied rage. Shards of glass that once protected my eight-by-ten senior photo predicted danger. Mark's dad, Jim, leaned in the doorway between the living room and kitchen, taking a drink of wine and a drag off his cigarette simultaneously. Half Apache, he had dark, brown skin, a square jaw, and a high, wide forehead. Even though I had seen signs of the power relationship between Mark's parents in my previous visits, I searched for something in Jim's eyes to tell me that he knew this wasn't right … or at least that everything would be all right. He never made eye contact with me during the ordeal.

No one spoke once the sealing-off began. Finally, Ruby stopped, took a long drag off her skinny, cigar-looking cigarette, and ordered Mark and me to sit down. Mark led me to an over-stuffed chair in the far corner of the room. He pulled me onto his lap right in front of the shade with the tear in it. Mark had told me stories of screams and threats, but I had never seen this private side of their family dynamics.

"So, big shot, how grown-up do you feel now?" Ruby said as she held out her wine glass for her husband to fill.

Mark wrapped both arms around my waist, and I knew I was being used as a shield of security.

"Mom, please, I just came to get my stuff."

"You think it's that easy? You just walk into my house, take everything I've ever given you, and you're out of here?"

"I'm just moving into an apartment, Mom. I'm eighteen. I'm not leaving you."

She paced back and forth. Her irritation grew when she realized she couldn't reach around me to get to Mark. Though I was a physical barrier, his parents looked right through me as if I were invisible.

Mark previously had described his mom's intolerance for weakness from her three boys and told stories about how she would encourage them to fight out their troubles. Parents were never targets. It was an unspoken rule not to do real damage to each other, and yet their interactions showed anger management was not an important skill. As a result, nearly every door and wall had holes punched at someone's fist level.

"Stand up like a man! Isn't that what you think you are? You stinkin' coward! Isn't that what he is, Dad, a stinkin' coward?"

At the mention of his title, Jim came to attention and swaggered over to join the debate. "A goddamn coward, he is."

With this, a grin formed across Ruby's thin lips. "If Mark thinks he's a man now, he should fight like a man. I say you and Mark fight."

She seductively glanced at her husband, coming onto him with a shake of her breasts.

"If you win, Mark stays. If Mark wins, he leaves."

Jim strutted around the room. Ruby gave him an encouraging pat as he passed. She smiled her most licentious smile, as if this subtle foreplay would summon his veracity and strength.

I prayed, "Please, God. Let something happen to stop this."

Out loud, Mark begged his parents, "Please! Stop! This is crazy!"

But they were both too deep into the bizarre ritual Ruby conjured up to be called back.

Jim took one last swig of his wine, held his glass high in a toast to Ruby, winked at her, and made his way across the pile of Mark's belongings.

"Get up, and fight like a man."

Mark made one last plea. "We'll just leave for now. I promise I won't move out. I'll stay here. We'll put everything back."

"Get up, you goddamn coward," Jim ordered.

Mark unlatched his hands from my waist. He protectively pushed me into the corner of the chair.

"Since I'm already a man, you take the first punch," his dad threatened. "Hit me! Hit me, you goddamn pussy!"

Tears rolled down Mark's face. His fists clenched at his sides. His father leaned into his face. Mark's shaking fist cocked back and struck his dad in the jaw.

Mark's dad never fully regained his footing as he stumbled behind his son's blow, across the piles in the living room. He landed near the front door. Blood gushed everywhere. It streamed from a deep gash across his forearm incurred when he landed on the shards of glass scattered like weapons around my photo.

Mark's brothers dashed out of hiding in answer to their mother's screech of instructions. They all left in a flurry to go to the hospital. We later found out Jim received seventeen stitches in his arm. Ruby said nothing to Mark on her way out the door.

Mark and I cowered in the dark corner. We held each other tight. Neither of us dared to move or even to cry. The beacon of light that previously entered through the torn shade had faded away as well. The room was completely dark.

When we were certain the headlights from the family station wagon had backed out of the driveway, we loaded Mark's broken and bloody belongings into his car. His white tennis shoes had blood on the toes from kicking aside the broken shards of glass near the door. Underneath lay the eight-by-ten photograph of me, a hole in it now where the frame's glass had punctured it. Mark picked up the photo and pulled the door shut behind him.

THE IN-BETWEEN

KIMBERLY JOY

I'd been laying in a hospital bed for two weeks. There was a war happening inside my body, and the disease was winning the battle. I lay curled in the fetal position, unable to sit or stand, eat, or drink. The vicious pain in my abdomen chewed on my insides like the teeth of a rabid dog. I pressed the button on the pump gripped in my right hand. Potent pain medication dripped into my vein. Warmth flooded my body.

As my pain ebbed, my mind drifted back to when I'd been diagnosed with lupus three years earlier, in 1999. Typical to my thirty-one-year-old type-A self, I had not slowed down, desperate to keep the life I'd always known. The one where I had a career, exercised daily, and traveled the world seeking out adventure. Looking back, I see that although my old life had kept me satisfied on the surface, it had also helped me avoid hearing the messages of fatigue my body was shouting. Not to mention a loneliness that resided so deep within me, I didn't even know it was there. I thought I'd been fully awake to life, but I had been disconnected from myself, others, and the mystical forces in the spiritual realm. Almost dying was about to change all that.

I had never worried about dying from lupus. I had thought I could beat the disease and continue with the life I had planned— volunteer in Africa, train for triathlons, fall in love—so I had never taken the time to grieve the life I was losing. I never really stopped to digest that this disease would not only change everything, but that it could kill me. And now, the doctors were desperately searching for answers, but I was declining at a rapid rate. My organs were failing. I was dying. I floated in and out of consciousness. Glimpses of an ethereal world that I would soon enter beckoned me.

A lightning bolt of pain ripped through my belly, jerking me back to the present. My jaw clenched, and nerve pain shot through my teeth. It felt as if two giant hands had squeezed all the air out of my lungs. I clicked the pump button again.

I bet others in this situation have places to turn for comfort. I did not. I had not grown up in a religious or spiritual environment. I did not pray nor feel there was something greater out there to comfort me. It's not that I didn't believe in God or a universal life force. To believe or disbelieve in something, you have to ponder its existence.

With each passing day, my physical body continued to weaken. The external world of hovering doctors and nurses, the beeping heart-rate monitor, the sensation of scratchy hospital sheets faded further and further from my consciousness. I didn't exactly know it at the time, but I was no longer fully in my body. That's when my otherworldly experiences began.

I frequently traveled to an ethereal place I now call the In-Between. I don't know what else to call it, because it doesn't have an official name. It's the realm of transitions, a plane of existence between this world and the next. For me, there was no white light; I did not go that far. Instead, I lingered for hours at a time in the In-Between, the expanse just beyond human existence, a sacred place where you exist as the True Self—Spirit or Soul. Words don't exist to describe it. But it felt similar to the passage from asleep to awake when you can still remember your dreams. Or like the quiet serenity of the Golden Hour, the time just before sunset when the light is soft and muted, the sun comforting and warm; or a day when the air around you is peacefully still, its temperature matching that of your skin, so you feel enveloped and at one with the expanse around you. In this dimension, time loses meaning. There are no sharp edges of anger or pride, no energetic tightness of shame or fear. There is only the open-hearted vibration of grace.

Usually, I spent my time in the In-Between floating effortlessly in a sea of profound tranquility and relaxed contentment. But one day, things began to solidify and take form. I was no longer in my hospital bed, but instead wholly embodied in the In-Between. I was sitting on the side of a *different* hospital bed. In it lay my dear friend Joel. Tubes protruded from his arms and chest. His face was swollen, and his head was shaved and bandaged.

❧

I'd met Joel in 1997. I had heard all about him from my friends. How he was handsome, smart, funny, could sing and play the guitar. Oh, and that he had brain cancer, for the second time in his thirty years. We'd met at his welcome-home party after his brain surgery. I was sitting outside in the hot summer night air, my legs tucked up beside me on a porch swing, when I saw him for the first time. He came out of the house; the porch light glinted off staples covering half of his shaved head. Dark circles under his eyes gave away his exhaustion, yet he took time to talk to everyone who came up to hug him and welcome him home.

I developed a huge crush on Joel. One night we had sat on my couch, touching and talking. Confused, he looked at me and asked, "What do you see in me? I'm going through chemo, am bald with a big scar on my head, my face is swollen, and I've gained thirty pounds from the medication." I was shocked. I'd never seen him in that way.

"What can I say? I love men with shaved heads." He laughed.

"But seriously, I only see you; your strong spirit, how you stay positive, and rather than complain, you live your life as fully as you can. You have wisdom and perspective on life that I respect. You're an amazing man." Joel leaned over and kissed me.

While my heart was open to a relationship with Joel, a few weeks later, he let me know he was not. As he'd begun to tell me that he liked me, my stomach sunk as I sensed the "but" that was coming. He'd told me he wasn't in a place to be dating anyone. He was exhausted and just trying to make it through all his treatments. He told me he was sorry but still wanted to be friends.

"Sure, of course," I chirped in my high-pitched sing-song voice that always emerged when I was pretending to be fine, even though my heart was breaking inside. We continued our friendship, but our time together became less frequent. Eventually, Joel and I lost touch.

⁂

Joel was still and quiet in his hospital bed. Then we started to communicate, miraculously, not through words; we just knew what the other was thinking and feeling. There was complete acceptance coursing between us. I felt free, unafraid to expose my heart.

I reminded him of the time when he'd wondered how I could want him with all his cancer treatment side effects, with all his "flaws" raw and exposed. I told him that moment was a preparation for me. I hadn't known I had lupus then. I hadn't experienced the medication, weight gain, hair loss, and other "flaws" the disease created. I thanked him for the gift of peace that conversation had given me.

"What peace?"

"The peace of knowing that even though I have an illness and all of the complications that go with it, I am still lovable. There will be someone who sees me, rather than my illness." He looked at me with love in his eyes.

"I'll always be here for you, Kim."

※

Our connection evaporated as I transitioned back to the physical plane. I was once again in *my* hospital bed with my throat dry and rough as sandpaper, muscle spasms making my legs jerk like striking snakes. My body felt tight and restrictive, as if I were trying to squeeze back into a pair of shoes that were too tight. But my cells had been bathed in unconditional love, and inside my chest felt effervescent, as if my heart had popped open like a bottle of champagne releasing thousands of tiny bubbles of love and joy. My Spirit was completely at peace.

The next few weeks continued to be harrowing. The doctors didn't expect me to survive. But after two abdominal surgeries and high doses of medication, I slowly began to recover. My fever broke, I started to eat again, and after a while, I was well enough to return home. As my health improved, I seemed to forget all about my time in the In-Between, rehabbing to regain my strength, checking a month's worth of email, and watching TV.

Six weeks after I returned home, some friends came to visit. We chatted easily about the Rockies game and Renee's new job. Then one of them said, "Kim, we have something we need to tell you." I could tell they were holding heavy news.

"What?'

"Joel died."

My heart stopped, and my mouth went dry. "When?"

"About two months ago."

"Why didn't you tell me sooner?"

"You were in the hospital when it happened, fighting for your life. We didn't think it would be a good time."

A slow dawning of memory began to form. It was wispy at first; then I remembered.

"Exactly what day did he die?"

୬ଽ

Later, I sat down with my journals and medical records, searching for what I was looking for. Chills moved over my body as I confirmed what I'd been sensing. The day Joel died was the same day I'd sat with him in the In-Between. We'd had a chance encounter, but in the end, he'd been going, and I'd been staying.

YOU'RE SCREWED

MISHA LUZ

I wish he would hit me. I was sitting in the garage, next to the washing machine, waiting for the load to finish. This was one of the few places in the house where I could steal a few minutes of quiet. The kids were running around inside the house and playing, the San Diego summer heat making outdoor play unbearable. He was inside too, assuming I was busy with laundry. I was smoking my cigarette, making every drag last as long as I could. Somehow, I had pictured my late twenties differently. I could hear their voices just beyond the door when the thought nudged me again. *I wish he would hit me. One good punch, just one solid shiner and I could leave. I would have an actual honest-to-goodness reason to leave. I wouldn't have to explain.*

I had been warned about him. Everyone saw the writing on the wall but me. The shame of having to admit that I made a mistake kept me in place, the burden of I-told-you-so's paralyzing me. Besides, I'm not a quitter. I have never *just* given up on anything. No, I had to make it work. *Just grin and bear it. Think of the boys.* My two beautiful, innocent, curly-haired boys who loved their daddy to pieces. *Keep your mouth shut and stay for them.* I took another drag. *How did I end up here?* I told myself it was because I loved him, but maybe it was more because I was scared and didn't know how to say "enough." The transition between "be a good girl, don't talk back" to "be a good wife, don't rock the boat" had seemed so seamless. But things had just gone from bad to terrible. Last week he almost did hit me. Me cornered in the kitchen, his fist right up to my face. He stopped right before throwing the punch. The kids had walked in on us.

I played the tape of our early days over and over in my head, trying to imagine a different outcome. He was charming and attentive at first. I was twenty-two, and he was thirty. He had salt-and-pepper hair, wore Armani suits and a Cartier watch, and lived downtown in a high-rise building. I had just left my family behind in Germany and was living on my own for the first time, trying to navigate college life in a foreign country. Everything about him seemed exotic and so grown up. I bought into his Suave Businessman image. Little did I know that one look from another man would shatter it, and a tsunami of rage would launch my way.

There hadn't been a shortage of red flags, but my fear of conflict outweighed the warnings. We argued about where I could go, who I could see, and what I could and could not wear. "You think I'm stupid?" he would often accuse me during rage-filled drunken arguments. He raised his voice, threw punches at walls, hurled objects across the room, until I learned to keep my mouth shut.

We tried therapy about a year ago. In the middle of our second session, he spewed outrage about how his laundry wasn't always done in a timely fashion. The therapist pointed out that his anger seemed disproportionate to the issue at hand and suggested that he could maybe avoid an argument altogether by doing his own laundry. He replied, "If I wanted to do my own laundry, I wouldn't have gotten married." He then got up and stormed out of the room. Our therapist, a middle-aged New York Italian man who had a knack for brutal honesty, looked at me and said, "I don't know what to tell ya. You're screwed!"

My dad had warned me about this. He said the burdens of life would magnify the problems in the relationship. I gave him my "I'm not a quitter" spiel. I was going to prove to him that I was a responsible adult, come what may. *I should have listened.*

Dad was sick again. His cancer had come back with a vengeance. *Now is definitely not the time to tell him about my petty relationship problems.* Over the next few months, I would travel back to Germany as many times as I could, trying to spend time with him on his last days.

I watched my father slowly disappear right before my eyes. By the end, he was completely dependent on help for even the smallest tasks. Seeing him like this broke my heart into pieces. My dad was my hero. He had never shied away from any challenge, but now, at the age of fifty-six, he was losing the biggest fight of his life. "Your mom took me to the Van Gogh museum in Amsterdam last year for my birthday. Can you believe she surprised me?" I knew he was in pain, but he had a big smile on his face. "We really made the last few years count, didn't we?" Mom held his hand and wiped a tear off her face. "You have to go after what you want," he would say. "No one else will do it for you."

This period was burdened with heavy, gut-wrenching grief, but it also gave me a way back to myself. I remembered who I used to be: a light-hearted and happy person. I used to know exactly what I wanted. I left my family behind at age nineteen and moved halfway across the world in pursuit of my dreams. I started to feel some of that strength percolating in my veins again. I was still my father's daughter.

After my father's funeral, I called my husband back in San Diego and asked him to move out before the kids and I came back home.

I was done fighting. Two weeks later, I returned home to find that he had refurnished our home with brand-new furniture, as if the problem with our marriage was hiding in the folds of the cushions on the old couch.

My breath caught in my chest. "I wanted to do something nice for you. I thought this could be a new start for us, you know?" I was trying to get away from him, but he kept following me around the house. "I mean, I know things have been a little rough lately, but we can make this work. *I* can make this work. I promise I will try harder this time."

I had just laid my father's body to rest, and with it, any capacity for another second of this bullshit. I told him that I would put the boys to bed and come back out so we could make a plan for his move out of the house.

By the time I resurfaced out of the bedroom, there were several empty bottles of beer on the counter. I walked through the house cautiously and found him in the backyard, sitting on a lawn chair. All charm had vanished from his demeanor. As I stood in the doorway to the yard, he turned towards me, his face ashen, his eyes sunken in. My blood ran cold when he opened his mouth to speak. "I don't know who you think you are, but you will not throw me out of *my* house. If you want to end things, *you* leave. And know that I'm freezing the accounts before you even get to the door. The kids stay here with me, and they will grow up to know that their mother abandoned them. I will not hear another word of this shit, YOU HEAR ME?! I am staying RIGHT HERE!" With that, he slammed his bottle on the patio table, sending foamy beer bubbles all over.

The image of my dad in his hospital bed flashed before my eyes. I heard his voice, clear as a bell: "No one else will do it for you."

I took a deep breath and looked up at the stars above, calling upon the universe to give me strength. Then I faced him, narrowing my eyes and keeping my voice cool and steady. "Looks to me like you are already *out* of the house." Before he knew what was happening, I stepped inside and closed and locked the backyard door. I calmly walked to the front of the house, grabbed his wallet, his car keys, and his briefcase, opened the front door, and threw all of it on the porch. Then I closed that door and locked it as well. I walked around the house, closing all the windows and pulling all the curtains shut.

First, he was mad, slamming his hands on doors and windows, cussing and barking at me. But once he realized that he had no way back into the house, he calmed and began begging and pleading. I finished unpacking and started a load of laundry. Then I poured myself a glass of wine and turned on the television. I let him squirm out there for a good while. He finally settled back down in a lawn chair and quieted. Before going to bed, I opened the door. He looked deflated and for the first time since we met, I felt connected to my power again. He must have sensed it too because this time, when I told him that my mind was made up, he didn't resist.

He moved out three days later, and I began putting my life back together. I had no idea how hard the road ahead was going to be and if I had what it would take to mend my broken heart and to support my kids the way they needed me to.

But I knew I wasn't a quitter.

MY FATHER'S HAND

AMANDA BYZAK

It was the summer of '89. I was twelve years old, had never been kissed, had not yet bled, and was Mommy's girl, a good girl. My parents had just divorced—the kind of divorce meant to punish, and it did. My mother left with nothing . . . but that was okay. All she wanted were her children.

She got us, all four of us, except for every other weekend. Her other prize? The decrepit two-seater Toyota work truck that had to be pushed to jumpstart. As the oldest, it was my job to sit in the passenger seat, twin babies on my lap, toddler at my side, and lean over and hold the steering wheel while my mom dug her feet into the ground, heaving that rusted old machine to life. Watching her struggle, I tried to push away the thought of being dead weight on her shoulders.

Before the divorce, we'd been poor, but provided for. Now we'd gone from poor to hungry. Hunger was a constant grating on my gut, consuming my day, like an obsession. Everything that I focused on was first filtered through these thoughts: *When will I eat? What will I eat? When will I eat again?*

Mom's minimum wage, scraped together with child support, got us a cheap roach-infested apartment in a bad neighborhood. My baby sisters and I slept in a small room on two twin beds pushed together. On the weekends, Mom cleaned a church in exchange for a box of food. "We don't take handouts," she'd say with fierce determination, staring into an invisible future only she could see.

Some might've felt embarrassed standing in that line, but hunger trumps shame. I loved that box of food like it was a Christmas present! There was peanut butter, jelly, bread, Top Ramen, canned veggies, tortillas, a tub of margarine, and dried milk to mix with water—not bad once you got past the chunks. I'd look at pictures in cookbooks as I ate.

My father kept our house. And in that house was a refrigerator filled with food. Real milk. Juice. Doritos. Meat-and-cheese sandwiches. Brand-name mayo. Ice cream. Kraft mac and cheese. Hot dogs. Hamburgers. Nesquik.

In that house, I had my own bedroom, a big TV, VHS movies, and a backyard. There were family events. Birthdays. Holiday parties. Cousins. Aunts. Uncles. Grandma. I tried to ignore the feeling that I was a guest, sitting on the margins of a happy family. I tried to ignore the desperate yearning to belong to them, while at the same time ignore the guilt of knowing, as I sat among them, my mother sat alone.

We had no family. My mother's family was filled with addicts, pedophiles, and criminals. She'd escaped long ago and wasn't going back. Her girls were her family and she, ours.

All summer, we were shuffled back and forth between our old house and the apartment, between having and wanting, between a bitter and vengeful father and a depressed yet desperately determined mother.

This particular weekend, my favorite cousin came to sleep over. My dad offered us his bed, and he'd sleep on the couch. I'd never slept in his bed before, so this was a special treat. His bed was built for a king, with thick wooden pillars and a flat wood roof, paneled with mirrors facing down. I used to lay across the plush velvet and satin comforter, look up at the mirrors and imagine one day it could be *my* bed. That night, my little sister, the toddler, slept between us. We giggled restlessly until we fell asleep.

I woke to a chill and a tickle.

The tickle was between my legs. I opened my eyes and looked up into the mirror above me. An image of a hand reaching across my body, tucked into my panties, came hazily into focus. *Whose hand is that?*

Oh, God . . . it's my father's hand! I lay frozen, feeling his fingers brushing the top of my pubic bone, playing with the first sprouts of hair, trying to reach further.

Abruptly, he pulled his hand away and ran from the room.

My heart pounded with a deafening swish in my ears, my t-shirt lifting slightly with each pulse. *He knows I'm awake!* I couldn't move. It was as though my true self had receded and the shell of me could not be commanded. I lay there feeling all of my body at once, like a passive observer. The heaviness of my frame sank into the bed. The skin he'd touched had an odd sensation that was meant to be stirred at a much later time, by someone who *was not* my father. A wave of shame hit me.

I stared up at myself. My image stared back, like a soul just departed, watching me from above. My oversized t-shirt, borrowed from him, had risen above my waist. *Did he pull it up?* The rest of me lay exposed. My panties, slightly lowered on my hips, bunched up across my pelvic bone, were stretched and askew. The exposure of my skin felt like I'd brought this on myself—as though my bareness was an invitation.

The deep breathing of my sister and cousin next to me grounded me in reality. I breathed out slowly, quietly. *This isn't a dream.* The alarm clock read 12:13 a.m.

I replayed the moment, and other memories emerged: my dad's face looking in through the bathroom window as I showered, him apologizing . . . "I didn't know you were there." *How many times did I not see him?* Waking to him standing over me . . . "You needed a blanket." *How many times did I not wake up?* Him staring into my dressing room while I was unclothed. "Don't worry; I can't see anything." Me, a little girl in the tub with him asking me to reach for a toy between his legs. My stomach lurched. *How could I have forgotten that?!* The memories were a patchwork quilt, the final square placed in its center, revealing the pattern. A question reverberated in my head . . . *Were you ever my dad?*

I heard him walk past the door, and my heart squeezed tight. I stood my post, staring out the window, hyperalert, waiting for morning to come, as if the light would protect me. As the sky went cobalt blue, exhaustion set in. Wanting to sleep, worried he'd return, I climbed over my sister to the middle of the bed, using her as my shield—a fact I am forever ashamed of. I pulled the blanket over us. *Will this be enough?*

I awoke, again, to a tickle.

The blanket was down. His fingers were running along the line of my panties on my backside. I jumped and turned over to look at him. He quickly gathered my sister, who was still sleeping, mumbled something about letting us sleep, and left.

This time I felt nauseous. *God, make this a dream.*

The day came. I hurried to play with my cousin outside and stayed gone until my mom came to get us that afternoon.

I told her that night. Aerosmith's song, "Janie's Got a Gun," came on the radio, a song about a girl being abused by her father. "Mom, this is a sad song, isn't it?"

She froze, looked at me, her eyes penetrating mine. One sentence and she knew. "That bastard!" Relief and dread filled me at the same time. Shouldering my burden, she paced the room in a heated debate with herself. "I'll kill him! . . . No . . . I'll turn him in . . . No, I'll kill him." I watched her, imagining each scenario, anxious to see what fate she chose.

He was arrested. He denied it. My mother pleaded with him to not victimize me again. *My God! He admitted it!* His One. Redeeming. Virtuous act. He went to prison and became a registered sex offender for life. I went to counseling. He went to counseling.

That sounds like a very happy ending.

But my father's hand did much more than my young mind could comprehend at the time. His hand had all but severed my relationship with his family, who rallied around him, first disbelieving, and later, after his admission, as his support. Favorite cousin, gone. Aunts, gone. Uncles, gone. Grandma . . . gone.

My father's hand opened a gate that wasn't his to open; it was his to guard. His hand had carved a father out of my life. In its place, so many predators came. Within a year, I lost my virginity many times over. I never learned *how* to say no. I never learned *why* to say no. I had learned I could endure anything. Endure . . . and recede. At seventeen, I became a dancer—and I don't mean a ballet dancer. I stayed in that life for seven years. I turned to women when I was tired of finding my father's hand among the men in my life.

It took a long time, but I have my own hands now. My hands have wrestled away his grip on the trajectory of *my* life. My hands have nurtured true intimacy in a husband, in children, and in sisterhood. My hands have reached within and pulled me back into the fullness of my being, a temple of joy. My hands have found strength through vulnerability. I embrace this world with my arms wide open; I bare myself to it. Can you see me? Can't you see . . . I am still a good girl.

STAVES OF STEEL

KATYA MCLANE

Note to the reader: This piece is based on the journals of my grandmother Mary Agnes Wilson, who was born in Tabriz, Persia, in 1892 and died in Montclair, New Jersey, at age thirty-nine in 1932.

For my sixteenth birthday, September 10, 1908, Mother invited all the neighbors to the party. But before the guests arrived, she said to me, "Agnes, I have a surprise for you." Her angelic smile made the dimple on her right cheek pronounced. "Come with me upstairs to my bedroom."

I followed obediently. *What could it be?* Perhaps a cape from Liberty of London? Mother drew the curtains and closed the door. My breath became shallow. *Why is she doing that?* Three large boxes from Macy's lay on her bed.

"Go ahead and open this one first." She pointed at one of the boxes.

I lifted the top off and rustled through the tissue paper. I gasped as I lifted out the beautiful satin chemise trimmed with pink ribbons and lace, then a matching pair of bloomers.

"They're beautiful." Then I giggled and added, "I'm glad I didn't open them in front of the party guests."

She nodded and said, "Open this one next."

Having gained some confidence, I didn't hesitate to open the second box. I stared for a moment, then looked up at her. "What is it?"

"It's a corset and a corset cover," she said. "It's time for you to dress like a young lady. I want you to try these on so I can give you a lesson on corset lacing."

I hadn't undressed in front of Mother for ten years and felt the heat of a blush as I stripped naked. "Put on the chemise and bloomers, then put the corset on by stepping into it and then pulling it up just under your breasts. I'll take it from there. It will take some practice for you to lace it up yourself. Stand in front of my mirror and watch as I lace you."

"There are so many eyelets to be laced, and the corset is heavier than I had anticipated."

"The staves are steel. Now, when you pull the laces of the corset, start from the bottom and work up to the waist." Mother busily tightened laces. "Now for the waist. This is the important part. You pull hard as you can to create the smallest waist possible."

"Oh! It's too tight. I can barely breathe."

"I know. You'll get used to it. Next, the corset cover. You slip it over your head and let it fall down over the corset. It keeps the laces and staves from showing through your dress. And now, the third box is ready to be opened."

I gasped again as I withdrew the turquoise-blue dress from the box.

"Now, just a pair of shoes and you are ready for the party."

I looked in the mirror and couldn't believe my transformed figure—my tiny waist and pushed-up bosom. *I've metamorphosed from a girl into a woman.* "I love my corset!"

Guests had arrived, and when I descended the stairs, all heads turned in my direction. Smiling, Father took my hand and murmured, "My little girl is a beautiful lady."

The dress and my corset accompanied me from Pennsylvania to Vassar College in Poughkeepsie, New York, and it served as my uniform for every dance. After I graduated in 1913, styles had changed, and I was living in New York City and going to Teachers College at Columbia. The Victorian corset with the tiny waist fell out of fashion, and the Edwardian corset put the waistline higher, above the natural waist—the Empire waistline of the Napoleonic era had become fashionable once again. *And I must look fashionable.*

A classmate, Dorothy Dickinson, told me that her father, Dr. Robert Dickinson, a famous gynecologist, had campaigned against the Victorian corset. "Father said that it damaged the female organs, making pregnancy and childbirth difficult. He never let me wear one," Dorothy said. "I'm so glad he was able to convince people that it was unhealthy. He thought it more sadistic than having women's feet bound, as they did for centuries in Asia."

The new Edwardian corset was still heavy, also with steel staves, but allowed more freedom to move and breathe. A saleswoman at Macy's on Broadway and Thirty-Fourth Street helped me fit my first Edwardian. "It makes your bottom stick out, and your head moves forward naturally to form an S shape," she explained. "But it slims the abdomen and thighs gently. I love mine. I can eat all the chocolates I want, and no one can tell."

"Why, that's perfect!" I said. "I love chocolates."

And I did. I could eat a box of chocolates in a day, which had led to my current dilemma. You see, my beau, Guy Converse, always brought a bouquet of flowers and a box of chocolates. Sometimes he brought me chocolate-covered caramels that were so addictive I'd finish off a box in an evening. Yes, I gained, but my "friend" the corset concealed it very well.

At least I thought so, until I went home to Pennsylvania for Christmas. Guy took me to the train station and gave me a huge box of chocolates, which I proudly brought home and took to the parlor, where the family was having tea when I arrived.

"You've gained some weight since we saw you this summer," Mother said. "Your cheeks are plumper. Anything to do with your friend and his boxes of chocolates?"

"Never trust a man who gives you flowers or chocolates," Grandmother muttered.

"That's why we wear corsets," I replied. "They are very good at concealing what chocolate does to the waistline."

Later that night, when I undressed in the room I shared with my sister Rose, I asked, "Do I look fat? Even with my corset on?"

"I think you look fine. Like one of those beautiful plump women that Raphael painted. From what I understand, plump is the preference now. It certainly makes your bosom look larger. I'm told men like that. The corset does reshape you quite a bit."

I loved my corset so much I gave "her" a name: Agatha.

In the summer of 1914, the Great War between the Central Powers and the Allies started. Guy could no longer get Belgian or French chocolates, only Swiss. *I am disappointed, but it will do.* In April 1917, Wilson declared war against Germany after German U-boats began torpedoing American merchant ships. First came the fear of the draft, then the realization of what it meant. We saw friends and family marched off to army camps in July, then rationing of gas and heating oil. The US War Industries Board, or

WIB, restricted the manufacture of anything made of steel, which was needed for guns and warships. The first restrictions were on automobiles and appliances.

"What will it be next?" I said to Dorothy Dickinson over lunch.

Dorothy smiled wryly. "Corsets."

"Corsets?"

"Yes, the staves of our corsets are steel. The WIB estimated 8,000 tons of steel goes into the manufacture of corsets each year and plans to announce the ban on corsets."

"That can't be!" But Dorothy was right. The WIB announced the ban the next week. The corset manufacturers retooled to make medical-corps belts and fencing masks instead.

Agatha can hold up until the war is over. I don't need a new one. It will be alright.

Walking down Fifth Avenue on a Saturday afternoon a few weeks later, two plainly dressed women stopped in front of me. "Why are you wearing a corset? Don't you support our men in the trenches?" one said.

"I think the Sedition Act, which makes it a crime not to support the war, should include those who defy the corset ban. I hope they arrest you and put you in prison," said the other. As I stood there, my legs frozen, the women walked around me and went on their way. I don't know what was more shocking: being accosted in public by strangers or that these strangers were talking about my undergarments. It was simply something decent people didn't talk about, much less in the middle of Fifth Avenue. After I had recovered, I returned home, shaken to the core.

The following Monday when I went to Columbia, again wearing Agatha, I noticed that the other women in the class were not wearing corsets. They gave me the silent treatment. That evening as I underdressed, I neatly laid Agatha in a drawer and gently smoothed her fabric cover, tears streaming down my face. "Agatha, I won't let them take you and melt you down for a warship or a gun. I'll hide you safely away." After that, it was like going out in public, partially dressed. Without Agatha, I felt insubstantial, unwomanly.

On Armistice Day, November 11, 1918, a newspaper article reported that the corset ban had saved 28,000 tons of steel—enough for two warships. *At least Agatha was not among those sacrificed.* I impatiently waited to hear that the corset ban had been lifted, but fashions had again changed as a result of the war. Corsets were out. I never wore my dear friend Agatha again.

SILENT STRENGTH

PATRICIA GEIST-MARTIN

I am eight, and I am terrified.

I stand with my two older brothers in the hallway outside my mother's hospital room on a cold February day in 1964.

I listen to a doctor in a white coat explain to us that our mom is sick; she has a bubble in her brain—a bubble that can burst if anyone upsets her. I don't fully understand, but I am frightened that I could kill my mother if I make a mess or don't do what she tells me to do.

The doctor says that, in addition to the bubble, Mom has a brain tumor, which they're hoping to remove completely with surgery scheduled for the next day.

But it turns out they can't reach the whole tumor without risking the loss of speech and other disabilities. Mom stays behind for radiation to reduce the part that remains. When she comes home a week later, I'm afraid of what the surgery might have done to her.

At home, though, Mom seems fine. When I return from school, she is there on her perch in the kitchen, asking about my day. She is there at the stove at dinnertime, dishing up pork chops and fried cabbage. She is there on the weekends to shop for a prom dress. She is there ready to plop down on the couch and listen.

She doesn't seem sick to me.

I am sixteen years old and feel carefree.

I walk in the door after school, calling out, "I'm home. What's for dinner?" and am met with silence. I wait for my mom's voice, usually in rhythm with mine, "Come on back to the bedroom; I'm sorting clothes." Instead, silence. I head to my room to drop my books, passing my parents' bedroom door.

And the door is closed.

My parents' bedroom door is never closed.

I stop at this barrier as if I have lost my way; I embrace my books, and swallow. Sounds of a woman sobbing come from behind the closed door. I don't recognize the voice.

The door opens. Marie, my mom's best friend, steps out. I make a quick duck-and-look move, but I see nothing before she clicks the door shut behind her.

"Your mom is just feeling a little sad today about things." Her round face and blue eyes move close.

"Sad about what?"

"Just things." She hesitates. "Don't worry." Her voice fails to calm me; it carries an edge that says there is nothing else to say, but she hasn't said anything at all. She reaches behind to turn the knob, opens the door just a crack, and slides back in. The door clicks shut with the finality of a judge's gavel.

I wonder if Mom is sick again.

I think of the hallway outside of her hospital room when I was eight. I think about the doctor in the white coat and his warning.

I don't knock. I don't ask to come in. I want to know, but I don't want to know.

❧

I am seven when her tears wouldn't stop.

My brother Bill and I round the corner on our block, heading home from elementary school for lunch, and we both chime "Wow!" "Look at all the cars at our house!" Bill bellows as he races ahead of me.

At the door, Bill pushes me aside, beating me to the finish line. The front door slams open as I jump to his side, both of us squished into the door frame, beaming.

Five unsmiling faces look toward the door, then turn back to Mom and Dad, huddled together on the couch, wailing, moaning—sounds I had never heard before in my life. Bill and I look at each other with wide eyes, then take slow, hesitant steps toward our parents.

"What's wrong?" I say, crouching at my mom's knees.

"What happened?" Bill asks, stepping to my side. "Why are you crying?"

Peggy, one of my parents' best friends, steps to my side, placing her hand on my shoulder.

"Your brother Ronnie has been in a car accident."

"Is he going to be okay?" Bill leans closer to Mom and Dad.

I slip behind Bill's shield. "Is he hurt bad?"

Clayton, Peggy's husband, moves to her side, and looks at us. "No, kids, I'm sorry—Ronnie was killed instantly."

I can't unhook my eyes locked on Mom holding onto Dad, both her arms tight around him. She supports him, as his back heaves up and down rhythmically. "Shhhhh sh shhh." Her lips purse gently, touching his left ear, a soothing sound. "Oh, Bill, Bill, Ronnie, our Ronnie, shhhh, sh sh," she repeats like a hymn's refrain.

The urge to cry bubbles up, but the shock caps it.

※

I gather up my books, push them tight into my chest, and walk in solid steps to my bedroom. Once I click the door shut, I listen again for the cry. Faint, but still there. I can't stop shivering. I stand frozen, as if holding still will keep tears from escaping the ledge. But one drops, and with it, my legs buckle, and I slip with my books to the pink shag rug by my bed.

I tell myself I can't cry. I won't cry. I must be strong for Mom. At least that is what I believed at seven, and eight, and sixteen, and then seventeen, when my mother died. We don't know why, but suddenly in October 1971, the tumor began to grow at a rapid rate, and two months later she was dead.

※

I'm twenty-nine, and I just found out that there is no heartbeat. This is the third time that the heartbeat of a hoped-for child has stopped. We were going to name her Hope, because that is what we needed to keep trying.

After the first, there was silence. My husband J.C. and I told no one about the second, third, and even fourth pregnancy. The pain of losing superseded the joy of telling. I stuffed it down and moved forward. And just like my mom, I am committed to not letting others see my fear, my devastation.

But the fourth was a charm. In the birthing suite, J.C. and I, with heads pressed together, lock eyes on this tiny four-pound healthy baby girl nibbling at my breast. We both inhale that powdery newborn scent and my lips are drawn into her soft, fuzzy, strawberry-colored hair. Inhaling all that is this moment, something in me shifts. Like time-lapse photography, I feel my inside strength blooming out and open for this little girl.

❧

I'm sixty-three, and my little girl Makenna is twenty-four. I decide that it is time. I secure Mom's medical record from the Mayo Clinic. It confirms my mom was admitted into the hospital on February 22, 1964.

The medical record fills in what my eight-year-old self did not know. An X-ray image revealed a "mass lesion" in my mom's brain, requiring surgery. After surgery, the doctor noted, "Unfortunately, a tumor involving the inferior portion of the left frontal lobe proved to be a grade II astrocytoma. Although the tumor could have been removed, since it was in the dominant hemisphere, I was afraid to risk it for fear of giving the patient a marked aphasia and possibly other neurologic deficits."

Reading these sentences is surreal. I'm transported in time; seeing and feeling what my dad must have felt. One year earlier, he lost his first-born son, and now this.

And I think about my mom—waking up to this news, hoping the tumor would be completely removed. I remember her losing all her wavy dark-brown hair to radiation, and how she took it all in stride, playing with different styles and colors of wigs, saying it was her time to be daring and try something new—perhaps even Marilyn Monroe blond.

I understand now from letters my mom wrote her sister, Gert, that Mom was in the business of shielding us from her worries. I scan to what she has written at the bottom.

> *I haven't written to a soul. I just couldn't. Please, dear,*
> *don't worry about me. I will be alright and will look*
> *forward to seeing all of you this summer.*
>
> *All my love, Ethel*

I read this letter and wonder if Mom didn't write, not only because she lacked the energy, but because writing would have made it all just too real—for her, for us. I wonder if this, too, was what upset my father. By not talking about her pain, her fear of dying, and her fear of leaving us, Mom pushed cancer to a backstory, a trauma that lingered like a lie pressing against all of us, shadowing our every move. Yet, the silence layered upon silence became a protective cocoon that served us well then.

I'm sixty-five, and I begin to question if the layers upon layers upon layers of silence is what was best for any of us.

THE GREAT ESCAPE

LYNN GAHMAN

He wasn't Daddy, of course. Nobody could be. But he made Mommy smile for the first time in a long time. And it was Easter, and he brought me the most beautiful gold satin rabbit. Geez, I loved that rabbit. Then he touched me funny, all the time saying, "Eh, what's up, Doc?" That's how it began, feeling bad and feeling good, all at the same time. No five-year-old could figure it out.

That was me, before.

It's 1968, the summer of love. That's rich. While my friends are primping for the prom, I'm sitting here, at sixteen, the youngest in the adult ward at Milford Psychiatric Institute. Institute. Geez, I love the sound of that. Like I'm getting a degree, not locked up for my own protection. Sounds weird, but I feel safe for the first time in years. Sigh. And just thinking that makes my heart hurt.

How did I get here? Even my friends at school don't know. There's a reason why kids don't tell.

"Hey, Mom, why's the ladder outside my bedroom window?"

"Jack," she calls from my room, "what's with the ladder?"

"I'm just cleaning the gutters. I'll move it." A couple of days later, the ladder appears outside my bathroom window.

"Jack," Mom yells.

"Just cleaning the gutters again."

We must've had the cleanest damn gutters in the neighborhood. I started changing my clothes in the closet.

Then he started with the pajamas.

"Jack, why are Lynn's PJs unbuttoned?"

"Beats me," he shrugs.

I don't say anything. I just want him to love me like my daddy does.

Instead, Jack keeps coming. Every night. In the middle of the night, he pretends to go to the bathroom, then picks up his toothbrush, and sets it down with the loudest click I've ever heard, to make sure she doesn't wake up. When I hear the click, I know he's coming. I try to slow my heart down, so he won't feel it beating out of my chest. I pretend I'm asleep. He pretends he believes it.

Ever since he started, I have the same dream: I'm running down a dark alley, gasping for breath, because someone's chasing me and gonna kill me, and I try to scream so that someone will save me, but no sound comes out.

I think maybe he's just trying to show me he loves me, the only way he knows how. I think, "Any family is better than no family." I can make this work. And nobody needs to know.

"Hey, Mom, I need a lock on my door."

"Oh, honey, *no* twelve-year-old needs a lock on her door."

Mom stuffs that right in with the mountain of other clues I've been leaving her. She's got a special mental closet marked "Do not examine."

I *know* better than to get pissed. Soon after they were married, Jack got mad cause I lost my hairbrush. He tossed my beautiful satin rabbit so hard; it knocked a sliding wooden door off its track. No telling what he'd do to me if I told.

But then Jack took his games to a whole new level.

Four a.m., I hear the click. Jack crawls into bed with me. I roll over, pretending to be asleep. He moves closer. I can feel his breath on my neck. I can't breathe. Jack keeps coming. I roll further, all the time pretending to be asleep. Now I've run out of space on the bed. And he's touching me. He won't stop. I don't even try to scream. No point. I just focus on the dogwoods on Uncle Max's painting, waiting for it to be over. Finally, he leaves. I want to take a shower, but that will wake everybody up. I try to sleep, but when I do, I always have the dream.

I've given up on giving Mom clues.

There's a reason why kids don't tell.

❧

Three years pass, pretending all day, every day, that I'm fine, just fine. Little Miss Achiever, head of the prom committee, member of the student council. Keeping up this happy family crap, all day, every day, is making me sick from the inside out. Mom sends me to a shrink. But nothing changes.

Months pass. I take to praying: "Dear God, please get me out of this." And darned if he didn't listen. I got busted for licking iodine off my finger to see if it would kill me. Who would've thought that would do it? I'd thought a lot about doing myself in, but, evidently, acting on it is a no-no.

So, I'm sitting here, in a red brick building with metal fence aprons around the windows, so we don't jump. It looks like a college for delinquents. My parents scrambled for a story. Officially, I "had a little upset" because there was too much pressure at school. As far as the hospital knows, I'm just "depressed with suicidal ideation." We all know our diagnoses here.

Most of us are in a kind of drugged-out suspended animation, hoping for—or dreading—visitors who waltz in, after they've pasted on their super-fake smiles.

I smoke a pack a day, pretending to inhale, arguing over soap operas on the only TV in the sunroom. ("No, Nikki would never divorce Victor!") Just trying to fit in with these adults.

But my hands have stopped shaking. And that "running for my life" dream? Gone. People are off their rockers here, but they're *my* people.

I can sleep now, even though I know Bob, the male nurse, will come in to check on me. Who'd have thought I'd ever feel *that* safe? Thank you, Lord.

Then yesterday, I heard a nurse say my insurance is running out. I've got five more days. I can't go home. I can't. I taste puke just thinking about it. I've gotta find a way to stay.

I see the shrink here ten minutes a day, three times a week. In all this time, he's had one moment of brilliance: he said I use humor as a defense, and it's not working for me.

This afternoon I did my best to flunk group therapy.

❦

Four days later, the meds have finally started kicking in, and they pronounce me "cured." I tell myself everything is going to be all right now. That it can be a whole fucking new chapter in my life. Like Cinderella. Jack will get it, what he's done, and he will stop. And we can be a happy family.

And I really start to believe it.

∂₹

We go on vacation the day after I got home. But instead of changing his tune, instead of getting what he's done, Jack spends the whole week exposing himself to me, in public, while swimming. I say nothing. If I do, what will happen to me? Will anyone believe me anyway? Will that rage he chokes down burst free?

I imagine him choking me.

There's a reason kids don't tell.

"Shit, it's going to be okay, I tell myself."

But I'm starting to simmer.

Soon as we got back, Jack came downstairs to gloat.

"Well, that was a fun vacation, wasn't it?"

He's daring me.

"Not for me," I mumble.

And then—with those three little words—he just . . . exploded.

"What? What did you say?"

We are looking at one another. Eyes locked. His stare is a challenge.

"You come up here and tell your mother what you said!"

I know what he's doing because he has done it a thousand times. He scares the living crap out of me, and I back down. That's our routine, and we are on the merry go round again.

He grabs my arm, nearly ripping it out, and drags me upstairs so I can be face to face with my mother. He's daring me to tell her who he is and what he has been doing to me all these years. He's sure I'll fold.

I kept quiet for eleven years. I kept quiet when they put me in the psych ward, when they took me on that whole psychotic vacation. I didn't say a god-dammed word. But somehow, when he grabbed my arm this time—I was just done. Inside I said, Not. This. Time.

"I'm done covering for you!" I say. "Mom, do you know what he does to me?"

And the truth is out there. In the air.

I can hardly breathe, but I feel better than I have in a long time.

And then the surprise of my life. It's not me that folds; it's him.

"You're right," he says. "I'm sick; I'll go."

I wonder if this could be happening. Could it all be that easy? Could he just go?

"No, stay," Mom says.

No surprise there.

And he stays.

⅔

I graduate the next year. But he *never* touches me again.

I go on to become a counselor for at-risk youth. Because I want other kids to have a safe place to go when they need someone to believe them.

Believe me when I say speaking up was the most terrifying thing I have ever had to do.

There's a reason why kids don't tell.

And there's a reason why I tell my story. Why I won't ever stop.

Worry about your daughters.

THIRTIETH REUNION

MARILYN WOODS

I broke a good boy's heart long ago. At least that's what those who remain in Texas say to me. I was never sure.

I haven't told a soul this story. Certainly not my genteel, charming mother who believed I was the perfect young lady. Never told my husband, a mildly jealous type. I never told my children, as I was consumed with modeling appropriate behavior. And my grandchildren? If I told them today, I'm sure I'd get a collective eye-rolling and perhaps a "So what?"

Johnny and I were outliers at North Dallas High School. Both tall and skinny, a bit shy, somewhat capable and fairly smart, but in the whole scheme of things—the cheerleaders, the jocks, the Student Council—we were irregulars.

It began with "Would you like a ride home?" and advanced to movie nights and basketball games. Our times together were full of teenage anxiety, adventure, and countless episodes of slow dancing and heavy breathing. My mother had skirted over the pages of the compulsory sex education book, a succinct session we were both glad to have over.

One Sunday afternoon, after church and chicken dinner with his family, Johnny glanced at me across the table. We excused ourselves, begging "studying for finals." Graduation loomed.

As Elvis sang on the car radio, I knew I was about to introduce my boyfriend to my frilly teenaged room, full of ruffles, my pink

Princess phone, and *Silver Screen* magazines. At slumber parties, my girlfriends and I styled each other's hair into Audrey Hepburn's updo or Grace Kelly's polished bun. Like artists at the easel, we made up our blemished faces with lipsticks and rouges in shades of peaches and cream, cherry reds, and pinks.

Within an hour, Johnny and I sat on the bed in my second-floor bedroom in Dallas. My parents were not at home.

We had sauntered up the stairs, both nervous, fidgeting and giggling. With a playful jab, he squeezed my waist from behind as we approached the landing. I responded with silly, restless laughter that went on way too long. Too nervous to turn around, I kept walking to my bedroom door. I wanted something. I wanted it with Johnny, but I didn't know what it was. Turns out, I didn't have to know.

Innocent enough at the start, I sat on the edge of the bed. As he guardedly sat down, I couldn't help but smile, looking at him against a backdrop of curlicues, flowers, and butterflies on the plumped pillows. I moved a little closer to him. *Is this the way to do it?* His eyes blinked rapidly. He rubbed his right hand up and down his thigh. I leaned over and took off my patent-leather Papagallos. An unnatural jumpiness darted back and forth between us. Minimal eye contact. Some frivolous chatter. Hard to say which one of us was more amateurish; we were both virgins. *What do I do now?*

No directions needed. Suddenly, we were going at it hot and heavy. Excitement, euphoria, elation, and fleeting feelings of embarrassment. *Oh, my God, this is so much fun.*

Then, like a supersonic lightning blast, at the most amped up, sexually charged moment, Johnny pulled out. I gasped and let out a whimper and tried to make sense of what just happened. Not a word was spoken. *Had I done something wrong?*

Johnny bolted upright, his face pale, his mouth open. He ran his fingers through his hair as he leaned toward me, trying to speak. Nothing. He stood over me, looking like he had witnessed a murder. He panted heavy, exaggerated breaths for a moment or two, fumbled with his zipper and then dashed off to the bathroom. I felt my body stiffen; I shook my head again. *Am I still a virgin?* A coldness covered my body. I heard the front door close downstairs.

Weeks later, we graduated; we played all summer long; we never talked about that afternoon in my bedroom.

Four months later, I left North Dallas High School and went to Texas Tech University in Lubbock. In November of my freshman year, I wrote Johnny a Dear John letter.

I never heard from him after that. When I thought of him, I often chastised myself for the abruptness of the ending. Over the years, the magnitude of how my careless teenage behavior could have altered my life gnawed at me.

I married the right guy, my soul mate really, after college graduation. I became a writer and an artist, had a career in broadcasting, raised children, and loved my life balancing career and family.

I did not become an unwed teenage mother. I had Johnny to thank for that.

My long-time best friend, Janice, persistently urged me to return home for a visit. I finally obliged, returning to Dallas for my thirtieth high school reunion, the first I had attended since graduation.

Ours was a typical high school reunion; the girls looked much better than guys, many of whom had paunches, pocket protectors, and bald spots, and loved Willie, Waylon, and the Boys.

After the Texas-sized barbecue buffet—smoky, spicy ribs and sausages, pulled pork, baked beans, and coleslaw—I looked across the room, and there I saw Johnny, a tall drink of water as my mom would say, sitting in a booth. The afternoon sunlight shone across his still-blond hair now sprinkled with gray. He sat beside his congenial-looking wife. *Does she know who I am? Has he ever talked about me, about our afternoon together?*

Several times I glanced Johnny's way. *Why was I looking?* One fleeting moment, he looked too. I quickly turned away, and when I looked up again, I saw him excuse himself and come across the dance floor toward me. It surprised me that my heart fluttered. I loved the way Johnny walked—a little bowlegged—a gait much like John Wayne.

He held out his hand. In a soft Texas twang, I heard, "Would you like to dance?" Johnny's gentlemanly style affected me, just like it had as a teenager. Eerily, "You Send Me," by Sam Cook, our song from so many years before, came on the jukebox. Johnny used to repeat "honest you do," a line from the song, over and over.

A slight shiver came over my body. Mentally, I replayed our senior prom, me in pale-yellow lace, him in black. His arms gently encircled me just like they did when we slow-danced together all those years ago. At first, we maintained a proper distance. I found myself turning toward his wife. *Was she looking?*

Over the thirty years, I had pictured this moment and rehearsed in my mind what I'd say if given this opportunity to right our teenage wrongs. As Sam Cook's ballad ended, I took a deep breath. "I hope you don't mind, but I would like to say something to you."

In his unassuming way I remembered so well, Johnny said, "Sure." He pulled me a little closer, giving me the courage to approach what I had thought about for three decades.

"Johnny, I have three awesome children. I got pregnant all three times instantly without planning. It seems I was very fertile." I bowed my head, speaking to my chest, uncomfortable and unable to look him in the eyes. Deep breath. I faltered a moment and then continued. "So many times, I have remembered that afternoon in my bedroom ... " His body tensed.

"Thank you for having the courage and presence of mind to not eject sperm into me when I was seventeen years old."

I heard him catch his breath. He turned away for a moment.

I continued, "Highly likely, I would have gotten pregnant that one afternoon, and you and I would have been on a collision course."

Johnny, slightly undone by my forthright disclosure, shuffled his feet as we stood in the middle of the makeshift dancehall, ducked his head slightly, and was momentarily silent. Then he stepped back, grinned sheepishly, looked me in the eyes and said softly, "Gosh, no problem."

Two months after the reunion, I was back in my office at the radio station on the West Coast when the receptionist announced a phone call. "Line one for you. Name is Johnny."

"I'm in Los Angeles at a hotel. I wondered if we could have dinner." A familiar drawl.

I was caught off guard, almost as if I was free-falling back into young-love hell. *What had I imagined my pronouncement of gratitude at that thirty-year high school reunion would do? I certainly didn't mean to encourage him. I just wanted to express heartfelt adult gratitude for something that altered the course of my life.*

I regained my composure and demurred.

Today, as my mind meanders over the memories of the moment, a tug at my heart suggests I may have left a little piece of it back in Texas on that sunny afternoon in May, a million miles ago.

A NEW STAR IN THE SKY

JANICE ALPER

Long Beach, California, February 22, 2009. The lifeless body of my thirty-nine-year-old daughter, my youngest child, lay faceup on the dirty bed, eyes closed, toothless mouth open, long blond hair fanned out on the sheets. Bones showed through her onion-like skin.

I looked at her and remembered the starry night years before when I told my husband about my dream of having twins. He joked and said, "Gemini." We laughed, but it came to fruition.

I turned to him at this moment and choked on my words. "She looks like corpses I've seen in pictures from concentration camps." We held each other and cried.

We covered her up, walked outside to Julie, her sobbing identical twin sister, and called the funeral home.

Sharon Marie Alper, born December 8, 1969, was the smaller and one-minute younger of the twins. Premature, they remained in the hospital for six weeks. Early on, we noticed troubling developmental signs, particularly with Sharon. She had frequent tantrums and often banged her head on the floor. She continued to crawl long after her sister could walk.

A pediatric neurologist shocked us with his diagnosis—chronic brain syndrome, or delayed development. This one sentence plunged us into years of special education.

At nine, Sharon had grown into a feisty child with a bright mind of her own. Despite her struggles, she wrote wild, wonderful stories about monsters and dragons in an indecipherable script as she listened to heavy metal. She made guitars from cardboard boxes and performed for the family. We all laughed and applauded. And worried.

Sometimes when I dropped her off at summer camp, I would fantasize that she might grow up to take her place in the world. I saw her as a strong, confident woman with a job and a family of her own.

But as she grew into a teenager, a different reality emerged. I remember being up one night at 3 a.m. Tossing. Turning. Unable to rest. Reliving the argument from a few hours back.

I had been standing near her bathroom, as I did many nights, and said, "The dentist said if you don't brush your teeth, they'll fall out."

"I don't care."

In the morning, I was groggy from not sleeping when I handed her fresh clothes. Yet when I saw her leave for school, she was wearing her clothes from the day before. She had pulled them out of the dirty laundry. I wondered why. I suspected, and I confronted her.

"Tell me what you are taking," I demanded.

"Nothing, Mom, I swear."

"Do you know kids who do?"

"You never believe me. Why don't you ask Julie what she takes, or one of my brothers?" and then she slammed the door. I stood frozen. *Am I being too demanding? Or am I looking away too much?*

What followed next was a downward spiral of smoking, unwashed stringy hair, dirty fingernails, and teeth falling out one by one. More questions surfaced. *Should I not have gone back to school? Am I repeating my mother's cycle, pursuing my own interests and becoming a shadow in her life?*

By the time the girls turned eighteen, Marv and I were just plain exhausted. We helped them get social security and moved them into a neighborhood board and care facility. We made weekly visits and took them out for meals. We clasped hands in hope. They made friends and went out to the coffee shop or movies as a group. Sharon's anger seemed to subside. Until Julie found a boyfriend and moved in with him, leaving Sharon at the facility on her own.

At twenty-one, Sharon was toothless and her cheeks sunken, similar to a wizened old woman.

Six years later, I received a call from the director of her facility. It was a call that severed all of our lives into *then* and *now*. "Sharon has been diagnosed HIV positive. She has to move."

The phone froze in my hand. "Are you sure?"

"Yes, we had her tested three times. We can't let her live here."

I gasped, speechless, and fought back tears. At the time, we were living three thousand miles away in Atlanta, Georgia, and I felt completely helpless. A broken record played in my head. *Why did I spend so many long days at work? Why wasn't I by her side more?*

When I called Marv with the news, the next thing that came out of my mouth was, "That's a death sentence. I don't want her to die."

"Don't get ahead of yourself," he cautioned.

We combed the internet and located a care center at St. Mary's Hospital in Long Beach and flew out to California the next day.

The care center was stark, sterile. Marv, Julie and Sharon and I sat in an awkward circle in the hard blue plastic chairs. An ever-present source of comfort, Julie reached out and held Sharon's hand. "Don't worry," she said, "I'll take care of you."

We looked up to find a young woman with a ponytail and clipboard. "I'm Vicky, Sharon's case manager. How are you?" I tried to smile back, clenched my fists, and braced myself for what she was going to tell us. Sharon stared at the ground as Vicky leaned in and began, gently, "Tell me about yourself, Sharon."

Silence. "I'll answer for her," Julie said.

I asked, "Should we leave?" thinking Sharon might do better without Marv and me in the room. But Sharon muttered, "Don't go."

We settled back in our seats, and Vicky discussed t-cell counts and viral loads. "What does all that mean?" I asked.

Sharon stood up, tears streaming down her face. "I'm really angry about this. My sister is the one who fools around, and I'm the one with HIV."

Vicky touched her arm. "Fortunately, we're living at a time where we can manage HIV, and people are not dying from AIDS anymore."

"Well, I don't want to hear this. Let's go, Julie," and the two of them stormed out of the room.

Embarrassed, Marv and I squirmed in our seats. "We really want to know what to expect."

A week later, Sharon allowed the tests and was prescribed a "cocktail" of drugs. We stood at the pharmacy, collecting one prescription, then the next. "Don't worry," said Julie, "I'll make sure she takes them."

I wasn't so sure. "How about coming back to—"

Before I finished the sentence, Sharon was halfway out the door. "No, I am going to stay here, and Julie will take care of me."

The medications seemed to work. A tiny sliver of hope we clung to.

Two years later, we were shocked at Sharon. Thin. Frail. A shell of her former self. I hugged her, and she hugged me back—

hard, clinging—put her head on my breast, and sobbed, "I love you, Mom."

"I love you, too, Sharon," I said. "Tell me what's going on."

Julie chimed in, "She hasn't taken her meds for eight months, and the doctor says she has AIDS."

I let her go as my knees started to buckle, and I searched for a place to sit down.

The nurse practitioner said, "Sharon, you need to take your drugs. It's life or death if you don't."

"Okay," she said half-heartedly.

"You know I take care of her," Julie said. I wanted so badly to believe it.

A year later, we returned permanently to California. Sharon had sores on her body and could hardly walk, and her skin was as pale as chalk. "If you take your meds, you will feel better," said the doctor. We filled prescriptions and left with heavy hearts, silent, each of us lost in our own thoughts as we drove home.

Only a few days later, her doctor called. "Sharon is here with me and not responding. I'm admitting her to the hospital." I couldn't swallow. By the time we arrived, she was in a coma.

With news that they were transferring her to the ICU, Marv looked up and asked, "What are her chances?"

"Hard to tell. We can try to resuscitate her, but we won't know if there is brain damage until we do more tests, providing she comes out of it."

I looked at the shrunken body, tubes feeding her, oxygen pumping, monitor beeping. So fragile.

A day after her thirty-eighth birthday, two days after the crisis, Sharon woke from her coma. True to her feisty self, she left the hospital and hung on for another fourteen months. She died in her bed silently one night, and I received the call no parent is truly prepared to receive.

The unhealed wound of her loss stays with me. Occasionally it festers; I reach for it, like an itch I can never scratch. Sometimes I beat myself up. Sometimes I close my eyes and remember my beautiful creative daughter. Sometimes I am unreachable, lost in the pain.

Early on, no matter what people said, nothing could provide any comfort. I found there were no words that could provide an ounce of healing until I heard this one philosophy.

A friend of mine shared the belief that when a person dies, a new star appears in the sky. The pain still stuck in my heart, but there was a shift, a modicum of comfort. As Sharon's ashes languish in a velvet case in my home, I think of her now as a star who didn't completely fade, after all; she just relocated to another place in the heavens.

GOODNESS THROUGH AND THROUGH

MARIJKE MCCANDLESS

1996. San Francisco, California. I was thirty-four years old, spending the weekend with my husband and a small group of people who were all participants in a yearlong "Love and Ecstasy" training designed to foster deeper intimacy. As it turned out, the training also included exercises to help participants heal from sexual trauma. We weren't your typical couple, and this wasn't your typical weekend.

My husband was working with me when I suddenly experienced a flashback that caught me by surprise. Although I had begun experiencing traumatic flashbacks some months earlier, I had little context for this particular experience, which was simultaneously horrifying and mystical—it was a moment that has stuck with me over the twenty-three years since. About a year ago, it surfaced again during a five-day silent meditation retreat in the Sierras, offering me an unexpected perspective that changed me forever.

The Love and Ecstasy training had brought forty of us together for three separate ten-day-long workshops over a year. In between those longer trainings, smaller regional groups gathered on weekends at each other's homes to practice what we'd been learning. On this day, our small group had finished formal practice, and we were beginning to chat when I was seized with the need to leave the social setting. My husband and I retired to a private room and continued to practice on our own.

The exercise we were practicing involved holding and releasing trigger points. The idea—much like how massage works to release physical knots—is that the body's private parts can hold stress and tension from unresolved trauma that might keep you from fully connecting with your partner. It was vulnerable work because healing also meant experiencing any trauma again—not only the physical sensation but emotions and memories.

Alone in our private room in San Francisco, the onslaught of flashbacks began. My body trembled from head to toe. I felt ready to bolt at the slightest motion—like a mouse suddenly aware of a nearby cat. I didn't understand yet that I was suffering from PTSD. I squeezed my eyes shut, though the flashes happened in my mind's eye: partial scenes, patched together haphazardly, each incomplete snatches of a small child's memories.

"There's a mattress on a dirt floor," I said, shuddering.

"I'm in a bathroom … but it's not the bathroom from my house."

"There's a Christmas tree and a picture window … but it's not my house." I told him.

My mind struggled to make sense, unsure if I could trust these visuals. I began to recognize that the scenes were from a neighbor's house whose layout was similar to ours, although it housed a mom, dad, and five kids, not two.

The flashbacks kept coming. I recoiled, horrified by the visual of a looming, leering grown man's face.

Suddenly the walls of the room fell into blackness. Instead of being a thirty-four-year-old mother on retreat with her husband, I was a small child, maybe four years old, in an unfamiliar bathroom.

There was a man. I knew this man. I trusted him, but now ... I feared him. I wanted to call out for my mother. *Mommy, where are you?*

Meanwhile, the adult woman in me raged. *How could he take advantage of someone so young?* I hated him. *Shame on him.*

But it was I who felt ashamed. I was naked and exposed, completely vulnerable. I wanted to hide, to huddle in a fetal position—to be told that everything was okay. I covered my face with my hands, unwilling to be seen.

My husband comforted me until I began to feel safe enough to continue. I took a deep breath as he gently took my hands away from my face and looked at me. While my eyes were shifty and unfocused, still wild with fear, his eyes were calm and present. He acknowledged my fear, gently encouraging me to stick with it with his strong, stable presence.

My flashback broadened enough for me to see the man's face— the dad of the five kids. Although older than my dad, he boasted a full head of dark unruly hair. His face was contorted.

Then, just as I was shrinking in fear, something extraordinary happened. I had a mystical experience that I have found hard to explain and have rarely talked about. It was an experience where definitions blurred, perspectives changed, and I existed on the edge of my known reality. Here's what happened. In one instant, I was that little girl, cowering. Then in the next instant, inexplicably, I flew into the man's perspective. I was now him. I was looking through his eyes down on the child who was me. I saw the scene through his eyes as if I were him. And stranger yet, I felt what he felt. And what he felt was desire. Urgent hot energy full of longing and passion flowed through my (his) body.

Then, just as suddenly, I was the adult me again, a woman on retreat with her husband. My own body stirred—an involuntary response.

What?

No! my mind protested.

Yes, my body replied.

I felt hot and aroused. My body was reacting, even as my mind tried to stop it.

Then, as if the edges of reality had not bent far enough, I was simultaneously all of us: child, man, and woman. I was the child, afraid and uncertain, trembling in the dark. I was the man, whose urgency overtook him, blotting out all reason, ruled by desire. And I was a woman outraged at him and at the circumstance, and betrayed by her body.

For a moment, I was not identified with any one of these points of view. Rather, it was as if I had stepped back and was calmly, without judgment, witnessing each of these three different points of view.

Then just as suddenly, I was somehow myself again—a thirty-four-year-old woman, still experiencing disparate things: fear and pain, anger and betrayal, yet aware too of the wetness between my legs. I flushed from my head to my toes, mortified. I wanted to disappear.

And the inner critical voices started.

I am bad.

No—wait. You are good. He is bad.

No, wait.

Who am I?

My body was out of control, and so too was my mind, running helter-skelter, searching for right and wrong, for good and bad.

My head screamed:

You must stay in control. If you can't be in control, you are like him. Bad.

The voices battled.

That's right.

You are bad.

No.

I am good.

He is a shameful perpetrator.

I am an innocent victim.

Wait.

What is shameful? Am I shameful?

Back into my own perspective, I was shocked to discover that what I felt at my core was neither fear nor shame. What I felt was deep, gut-wrenching compassion.

He, too, was responding to his body—to his conditioning.

Was his behavior worthy of punishment? Yes. Certainly.

But …

But what?

The experience pushed me to ask questions I never had before, like What else is here?

Do his acts define me? Do mine define me?

These questions stopped me in my tracks.

And left me fundamentally curious.

Who am I?

❧

It's a question I have carried with me since that day when I lost myself—when I couldn't tell if I was a confused woman, an innocent, scared child, or a lustful middle-aged man. A day when I was inexplicably flooded with compassion for each.

It's a question I take with me on silent meditation each year. It's a question that I have been investigating for twenty-three years.

ॐ

The question remained until 2017. The Great Space Center, Lone Pine, California. We were on our annual silent retreat when something broke loose. In one shining moment, I saw the truth.

What I saw was something unsullied and inviolable—an intrinsic purity that was fundamentally good, despite a broken covering. I saw that each of us—rapist, child, woman—has an intrinsically pure golden core, actions notwithstanding.

I am not bad—no matter what I do or feel or think. I am not bad, no matter what happens to me.

And in seeing that, I saw something else, something hinted at that day long ago. Something I was not ready to accept then.

Could it be that maybe he is not bad, either?

Could it be that he, too—despite his heinous, punishable actions—is intrinsically good at his core?

Could it be that he is a perfect reflection of me?

That I am also a perfect reflection of him?

Could it be that we are all One?

—*exactly* the same naked awareness

—covered and hidden by the delusion of our particular conditioning.

And then, eventually, I saw it perfectly—the thing we really do not want to say.

Today, twenty-three years later, I speak it aloud:
"You, perpetrator
I see you. I feel you.
And I wish you
no shame,
no judgment,
no retribution,
no righteousness,
no fear.
I forgive you.
Because
I am you.
And I am goodness through and through."

THE BLACK BOX

HEATHER M. BERBERET

I had always believed that at some point in my life, *talking* would be the thing that would eventually reconcile my mother and me. In my fantasy, she would say she was sorry for the lying, the untreated depression, the alcoholism, and the years of silent treatment after I came out as a lesbian. I would apologize for my ingratitude, for ignoring the sacrifices she made for my sister and me, for the education she never got to use.

I did not, could not know that reconciliation would happen in a quiet moment as she slowly died, bound in the same silence that had characterized so much of our relationship, all because of my sister's baby book.

A small thing in the course of a life, but that book, seeded into the soil of family dysfunction, sprang up between my sister and me like a persistent, prickly thistle-weed. As the story goes, I tore it up and flushed it down the toilet when we were kids. I don't actually remember the book, or flushing it down the toilet, but who needs memories with a family that re-tells your most embarrassing story at every gathering?

Without a baby book, my sister's infancy disappeared, creating an emptiness that has haunted both of us for decades. I have felt terrible guilt, believing my actions were personal, deliberate even—an expression of rage at her intrusion into my life.

In college, during my first round of psychotherapy, I demanded ownership of my baby book from my mother. After months of delay, she eventually handed it over but insisted that it still belonged to her. That pissed me off. Her alcoholism and depression had robbed me of the childhood I deserved. What gave her the right to rob me of my memories, too? But, as she often did, she kept her truths to herself, offering no explanation. I didn't give the book back.

My baby book is forty-nine years old now and falling apart. The protective plastic cover is yellow and brittle. The binding cracked after being crammed with so much stuff, like the lock of golden-blond hair living in an unmoored security envelope.

Inside, my mother's beautiful Catholic-school-girl writing covers the pages. She took a lot of notes my first year, each photo accompanied by pithy captions like, "My little prizefighter." When I look at the book, I imagine her sitting down with a cup of coffee at our antique kitchen table while I napped, filling in the blanks, documenting our lives.

I searched the book for my angry child-self who had torn up her sister's book. Instead, I found a pixie-haired elf of a girl who smiled a lot, especially when she held her baby sister. I didn't look like the difficult child I had believed myself to be. And still, the history of the other, lost book and the rift it caused between my sister and me created a hard peach-pit of a knot deep in my gut. So, I put my book away, avoiding it like the squeaky step on the chairs, until my mother was diagnosed with multi-system atrophy.

Over four years, she lost the ability to move as her brain stopped making dopamine. By the winter of 2011, she spent her days confined to her bed or a wheelchair.

I yearned for my imagined moment with my mother before she died. When, despite my attempts at communication, it didn't happen, I unconsciously sought out another relationship to fix. That year, my sister both turned forty and got married. I decided to track down some photos and, come hell or high water, gift her with a goddamn baby book.

Despite begging family and old friends for photos of my sister as a child, I didn't get a single one. Desperate, I asked my mom. Surely, somewhere in a dusty corner, a few leftover pics judged inadequate for the original book, remained. But again, she delayed. She excused. With only a few months until the wedding, I demanded. Finally, she relented.

"There's a box in my closet. It's black, up on the top shelf." Pause. "There are a couple of them." Sigh. "Take what you want."

Thrilled and relieved, I climbed the stepladder and peered into the dark, dusty crevice of a shelf. I had assumed I would find out-of-focus, over-exposed, photographic dregs, abandoned in film-processing envelopes from the 1970s. Instead, I found *tons* of photos of my adorable baby/child sister with curly blond hair, pouty lips, and a cute upturned nose.

Once the photos were placed in the new book, I started spending time sitting in a chair next to Mom, talking through them one by one. While she gave me names, dates, places, and anecdotes, the miracle of that time was how it felt to be with her—long, quiet afternoons together, without the buzzing distractions of electronics or life business. Dad, working in his study, would amble into the bedroom whenever Mom couldn't remember a detail. He'd sit at the end their bed, and we'd talk about our shared lives. This is the only memory I have like this, my parents and I, joyfully remembering our time as a family.

Toward the end of the process, I wrote the caption for a luminescent photo of my two-year-old sister, sitting alone on the beach in a bright-red one-piece swimsuit with frills, building sandcastles with a pink bucket and shovel.

It was such a beautiful photo I said to my mother, "It's strange you have all these great pictures of her. You must have taken so many for *these* to be the leftovers."

She looked away, silent, a silence as familiar to me as the smell of her perfume. All at once, I knew. Like when you finally solve a difficult math problem or dream in a foreign language for the first time. A moment of gestalt.

There had never *been* a baby book. She had never made one. As a mother of my own young child, I understood. Second children rarely have a full-fledged baby book; there's no time. Or my mother was too depressed, too lonely, too drunk to make one for my sister. She told a lie on the fly, not thinking about it, not intending any harm. And still, she had birthed a lie and then protected it through silence. The longer it lived, the harder it was to kill. Ultimately, she sacrificed my only sibling relationship to hide her shame with a lie so small, yet so critical, it shaped the future of our family.

I stopped breathing as anger threatened to wash away every sweet moment we had spent together over the previous weeks. Nothing had changed. We will never reconcile. She will die, and our story will end here.

As a naive child, I had believed her explanations. This time, as an adult, I was just too scared of the intimacy of honesty to speak. I swallowed my anger, afraid of both her denial and her acknowledgment. I froze and joined her in the lie.

That was the last time my mother and I met to talk about the book. A few weeks later, I presented it to my sister on the morning of her wedding. Surrounded by beloved women, my sister spent time with each page. It was obvious she liked it and, while I hadn't repaired the damage of all the years, the book helped, serving as my white flag of peace, my gesture of reconciliation.

It's been seven years since my mother passed away and, unlike her, I've had time to play out this story over and over. I realize now that, regardless of why I didn't speak, we did share a moment of grace. She was dying, running out of time. Forcing her truth into the open would have changed nothing about our past or my future. She was, in all ways possible, paralyzed. And so was our relationship. Healing, that shift between us, came with the gift of my silence. For her, one less moment of shame to carry into death. For me, a moment of redemption to carry throughout my life.

LOVE AND LIES

SARAH VOSBURGH

The lie was told with equal measures of angst and self-loathing. Looking into the confused, fearful face of my mother, who peered back at me with an unmitigated hope that I would make things better, I had never felt more unlovable and less trustworthy: betrayer that I had become. It had taken weeks of planning with many little lies along the way, leading to this mockingly beautiful day with a cerulean sky and the excited reds, yellows, and oranges of New England trees against my black and petrified heart. There was no hope now. No turn toward the future where there might be even a suggestion of hope for improvement or a twinkle of joy in recognition. We'd entered a dark, spikey cave where behind-the-entryway sealed us in, and there seemed to be no exit beckoning ahead.

We were on our way to the memory-support facility, misnomer that it is, and I had lied to my mother to get her in the door. This is a door she would enter, and after doing so, she would never return home. After this she would never again cuddle at night with her kitty, or make herself a cup of coffee and forget where she put it, or soak in a tub full of lavender bath salts to wash away her cares and relax, or shuffle down the hall to her bedroom closet to find her favorite sweater against a chill that wasn't there, or answer the door delighted to see the faces of her granddaughters whose names she could not remember, with her bra on over two sweatshirts.

This particular morning came after weeks of paperwork and the interview with her that had to be held at a local restaurant else she'd not have gone. That was the interview held with her then-husband, where they noticed how she cowered from him and jumped when he gesticulated, after which they called me. They were as sure as could be that the increasing bruises we had all noticed were the result of his abuse and not her clumsiness. They had moved up her admittance for her safety. Try that on for size. Here I was working desperately to help my mother maintain her independence, thinking she had the support of someone who claimed to love her, only to find frustration had got the better of him, and she was at the bruised end of it.

I had pulled out favorite items from her laundry to place in her small closet in her small room with the necessities but nothing else: a single bed, night table, and chair, and a small bathroom with a shower. I could count the number of times my mother took a shower in my lifetime on one hand. She preferred baths. This small fact tortured me. She sang in the bathtub, her clear straight tone giving voice to spirituals and folk songs. She always came out renewed and refreshed. The facility didn't have bathtubs.

I had taken knickknacks and blankets and artwork from her home I thought would provide her comfort and familiarity in her new surroundings. I bought new sheets for her bed with Snow White on them, because these days it was a movie she loved to watch over and over. I arranged for flowers to be delivered weekly to her room for her night table, and a monthly seasonally related wreath for her door. I had to get special permission for that. But unlike other plain doors with institutional nametags on them, hers would be discernable immediately to her and to the others whose company I romantically hoped she would come to enjoy. Earlier, when I went to visit the place in my hunt for an appropriate one, I ran into two old ladies from church. I had wondered where they had gone off to. The same fate, I guess. Familiar faces—not that it would make a difference for my mom, who, on a good day in her youth, had trouble recalling faces.

She was glad to see me when I arrived to pick her up that day, and even though she didn't recognize me, she knew she trusted me. I took full advantage of that trust and lied. She couldn't remember where we were going or what we were doing. So, I spun the tale, the complicated and compounded prevarications rolling off my tongue. I reminded her that it was critical to get her blood pressure under control, and I thought a stay at this place would be preferable to time in the hospital instead, which the doctor had said (he didn't) would be necessary to find a way to regulate her pressure. In addition, the facility needed someone to do workshops for the old folks on flower arranging (they didn't), and she was just the florist to do it.

While she had been a sought-after presenter on flower arranging at garden clubs, junior leagues, and libraries just a few years before, at this point, she could barely keep a conversation going for three exchanges, let alone plan to teach others. She argued with me a bit about the blood pressure thing and kept asking why. I repeated the lie so often, so lovingly and carefully, that I almost believed it myself. And she bought it for the time necessary to get her in the door and meeting folks, mostly because she was distracted by the opportunity to spend time with me even though she didn't remember my name or our connection.

They told me to stay only as long as was necessary. I wasn't to help her find her room or let her know of the creature comforts I had painstakingly imported for her comfort. No, I was to stay to introduce her to the head nurse, and the director whom she had already met but did not recall, and perhaps facilitate getting her involved in an activity, and sneak away. I was to abandon my mother without even saying goodbye. The latter I did not do. I let her know I was leaving, and that I would be back. I implied I'd be back to take her with me, though I never said so. I just let her think it; another prevarication, another lie.

My formerly fierce, smart, competent, kind mother looked at me at that moment with a mixture of acquiescence on her face and sheer dread and confusion and an unexpected but distant twinkle of recognition in her eyes, and she told me she loved me.

The resignation, acceptance, and love hit me at that moment out of the cerulean-blue morning, piercing my black and petrified heart. I finally spoke the stark and solid truth: I love you too, Mom.

MOTHERLESS

LAURA MAY

Asilomar State Beach is a one-mile beach with rocky coves on the Monterey Peninsula. I've always admired the jagged coast filled with crabs, starfish, and kelp beds. I'd spent the morning walking along the sandy strip, looking for a cluster of smooth rocks to serve as a seat. Asilomar means *refuge by the sea*, and I sat on these rocks, breath mirroring the tide, hoping to find refuge from my feelings of inadequacy because I have failed at becoming a mother.

Thoughts of my own mother, who had passed away nine years earlier, floated through the waves. I was four years old, and we sat on the stoop of our home in Long Beach, watching the fireworks on the Fourth of July. I looked up at bursts of red, yellow, and white. We sat knee to knee, holding hands in the darkness. I knew at that moment that she was mine, and we clicked like puzzle pieces. We fit. *Would I ever click like that with a little one of my own?*

It has been 273 days since my last miscarriage, the third miscarriage in less than two years. I've met with my own doctor twice and with a naturopathic doctor once, and I've had two consultations with IVF doctors. During these 273 days, I've also attended twenty-two therapy sessions and fourteen acupuncture treatments, and I'm taking nineteen supplements a day. Since my most recent miscarriage, my life has been dissonant, a never-ending path of valleys and peaks. I wander down to self-hatred and inadequacy only to rise up to compassion and self-care.

Some days, I think I'm a fool for taking all these supplements, and I roll my eyes as I listen to my therapist talk about "self-compassion." Other days, I feel strong and can accept my losses and acknowledge my fear that I may never become a mother. On mornings like this, I have focused on the sea, watching its subtle changes, wondering if I will turn like the tide. I recall each miscarriage and the feeling of unbearable grief, letting the memories drift in and out with the sea. I began to think about our first miscarriage in October 2016.

My husband and I were on pins and needles, so eager for our first prenatal visit. It had been six weeks since our home pregnancy test, and we were finally going to see the first images of our baby. Parenthood was becoming a reality. I had already circled our baby's due date on our calendar, a bright red circle around a seemingly uneventful Tuesday in June.

At the prenatal visit, we learned the fetus wasn't growing. "No growth. No heartbeat," said the doctor. I stared at the ultrasound screen, trying to see a baby, but I just saw this little pearl. A tiny pearl in a black hole.

"I'm sorry, but this is not a viable pregnancy," she said flatly. She then proceeded to schedule a D&C, an acceptable medical term for abortion, ending this pregnancy and the new addition to our family. My husband and I were silent in disbelief. I felt broken and numb. I was beyond angry, with no answers and no one to blame. In my mind, I kept thinking, *I am pregnant today, and tomorrow I won't be.* The next day, I checked into the hospital with a brave face and left that evening, guilt-ridden that I had ended my pregnancy. We had no choice, but it still felt like the worst decision of my life.

When the D&C was over, I tried to feel comfortable in a body that didn't feel like my own. I laid on the couch, watching reruns of *Law & Order.* I remember thinking that I should take a shower or check email, but I didn't have the energy. My emotional doppler radar was searching for some bit of optimism to pull me out of bed, out of my head. My body had failed me. The possibility of creating a bond like the one I had with my mom, to be connected with her again, was gone. Why wasn't she here to console me? No one talks about miscarriages.

After the D&C, the doctor urged us, "Don't wait. Keep up your prenatal vitamins and try again." Her words felt like a cruel joke. *Try again? Don't wait? Does she know what it is to be pregnant and hide it from your boss? Does she understand that I can't possibly put my body or our hearts through this again?*

Back on the beach, I sat on these cool, flat rocks, continuing to breathe with the tides. Taking deep breaths in, in rhythm with the ocean, exhaling as the water retreated from the shoreline. The coast had always been soothing. But not today. I sat quietly and was flooded by memories of the second baby I lost, another baby slipping away with the tide.

After that second miscarriage, I saw a couple snuggling a beautiful baby at my local coffee shop. The baby was the size of a bag of flour. His head was covered in fine hair, like golden threads. They cooed at him. They sipped their coffee, newborn in tow, happy. They were, of course, unaware of me. I examined their every move, obsessed with their family bond. I was elated for them, but it was creepy because they were strangers. I wanted to approach them, to find a way to morph into their world, but I was stuck to my chair, brimming with jealousy and hurt, my only companions. I envisioned myself getting up and taking their baby, casually walking out with him as though he were my ordered coffee.

The sound of a gull drew me back to the beach. I watched the crabs dance in kelp beds, busy with the morning. The rocks were smooth from the ocean's persistence. The waves crashed along the shoreline, creating a predictable melody. As I listened to the song of the ocean, I wondered if we would ever find our family rhythm. Everything was in concert with the tides, while I felt so out of sync. I longed to become a mother, and our third miscarriage made this possibility seem unattainable.

I thought it was a sign. Maybe the universe was telling me that living a life without a child would be easier than having a baby without my mom.

Looking out at the horizon, I thought about being pregnant for the third time; I was confident, even secure. I had all the typical pregnancy symptoms: exhaustion, nausea, headaches. This pregnancy felt different than the others; emotionally and physically, we were ready to have a baby. We were cautiously optimistic. The third time was the charm.

I was seven weeks pregnant when I started having horrible cramps. I left work early, blaming my departure on bad takeout, and I began bleeding. I remember this moment so vividly because I knew physically what was happening but, emotionally, my heart couldn't fathom it. I was sitting on the toilet, tears brimming, watching what we had hoped for go down the drain.

I remember waking up in the middle of the night to go cry in our guest room. It was the type of cry that was silent and felt in your abs. The deep pull of your muscles—as though you were excavating a pain so deep inside of you, it took everything to get the strength just to try and get it out.

After that miscarriage, I didn't miss a day of work. In fact, I went on a five-mile hike I had planned with my friends for that weekend. I was exhausted, my body hurt, but I did not stop. I felt like a failure and refused to acknowledge my loss. My co-workers didn't notice anything different, and neither did my friends. This helped me bury my grief. This was not something to talk about; the problem was me.

So, I was referred to an infertility specialist; the start of another long road. I didn't even like the sound of it. I wasn't infertile—I could get pregnant, but the fetus didn't grow. My body didn't hold onto these babies, and I didn't understand why. I thought my body wasn't strong enough or I was too old. Every time I asked a doctor, I got the same answer: "No one knows why miscarriages happen. It's unexplained, but it's not your fault." It felt like my fault. *How come my body couldn't do this?*

I spent many sleepless nights looking for answers: Should I be a vegan? Lose weight? Was I too old? Why did we wait? I beat myself up.

My mind was stuck in a vicious cycle of self-blame and worthlessness. I wasn't good enough to be a mother. We wouldn't try again.

I listened to the sounds of the ocean. A calmness came over me.

It was time to let go. Of the losses. Of blaming myself.

Shedding heavy coats of pain, I honored each loss and envisioned them getting swept away in the tide.

The sun broke through the fog, and I felt a warmth by my side. It was my mother sitting next to me. She held my hand, inviting me to have the courage to try again. "I'm scared," I told her.

"I know," she replied.

And then something magical happened. I just knew we would try again. I didn't know how it would turn out, or what the future would bring, but I knew my mom would be holding my hand the entire journey.

WHY WOULD ANYONE?

SUSAN F. KEITH

"Why would anyone be interested in working with people with schizophrenia?"

The snarky comment, made by my colleague at the Georgia high school where she and I were teaching, was meant to be a put-down. It was in the early seventies, and I was about to marry Sam, a smart, dedicated psychiatrist whose specialty was working with people who struggled with schizophrenia. At the time, I had no comeback, even though I'm not usually at a loss for words.

Truthfully, before Sam, I had never thought much about schizophrenia. But if I had, the images that I conjured up were probably of scary, possibly dangerous homeless people, disheveled and hallucinating. I knew that this was the way most Americans saw people with schizophrenia. My education began soon after we were married when Sam went to work at the Center for Schizophrenia Research at the National Institute of Mental Health in Maryland. His job involved reaching out to the community. Unlike other psychiatrists who were cloistered in research labs or tucked away in paneled offices, Sam sought to engage with the families of people with chronic mental illness. Although I was interested in Sam's work, I knew very little about it. I was a newlywed setting up our new home while adjusting to life in the DC area where everyone was caught up in the Watergate scandal.

One morning Sam asked, "How would you like to spend the weekend in Norfolk? I've been invited to speak at the Northern Virginia Schizophrenia Association."

A nervous sensation grabbed me. I wanted to go, and yet I felt inept. I knew I would be placed in a situation where I would be talking to family members. *How would I know what to say? What if I were speechless, once again?*

A week later, I found myself in a large conference room, watching my husband present the latest findings on schizophrenia to a large group of families. During a break, the woman sitting next to me said, "My son sits in his chair all day watching television. He's not even really watching it; he just stares at it. I try to get him to do errands with me, but he doesn't want to leave the chair. He's afraid he might miss an important message." I didn't know what to say, so I listened. It was easy to be attentive and sympathetic—the attendees were so heartfelt as they opened up—yet I was reluctant to comment. *What if I said the wrong thing?*

Realizing that I was Sam's wife, another mother approached me. "I'm so worried about who will take care of my son after I'm gone. It's something I worry about all the time." The pain was etched on her face. I nodded, listened, and felt I hadn't really done much at all. And yet her eyes spoke, full of gratitude. She thanked me. I realized the simple act of allowing them just to tell their story out loud was not something the families could do easily with the outside world.

Back at the hotel that night, Sam asked me what I thought. "It's not easy talking to the family members," I said.

"What's so hard about it?"

"Well, it wasn't really conversations. It was as if a valve were opened, and the words just poured out. I didn't know what to say. Dealing with schizophrenia day in and day out is numbing, terrifying. I got exhausted just listening to their stories."

As I closed my eyes that night, I realized my life perspective was shifting. The small hassles I encountered were nothing compared to what those families were experiencing. My hassles get resolved; their situation was unrelenting.

As we drove home from Virginia, I looked out the window and felt grateful I could be there, and yet I couldn't help wondering, *Would I ever become comfortable talking to people affected by mental illness?*

Three years later, Sam was invited to the first meeting of what was to become the National Alliance for the Mentally Ill (NAMI). For the first time, families would have the opportunity to get together to discuss their concerns. What was most exciting for Sam was that they would have direct access to resources and support. "If we're going to make any progress with this illness, we need to involve the families," Sam would say. At the time, many psychiatrists believed dysfunctional families, and especially "bad mothers," could cause young people to develop schizophrenia. As a result, most families had a natural distrust of psychiatrists, who they felt blamed them for the illness. As one of the first psychiatrists to attend the meetings, Sam represented "the enemy." He was heading into a minefield, and I was right there with him.

When we walked in the room, we felt that initially, they approached us with hesitation. But within minutes, their suspicions were dispelled. We loved watching what was happening as more and more families were truly understanding the diagnosis and gaining access to their local resources. We fell into our respective roles. While Sam would speak to large audiences, I would hear from individual family members. I was happy to listen, as I had realized that not talking about schizophrenia had only added another burden to their already full plates. I felt something was blossoming in me and in the families with each interaction. As I listened to them, I gained their trust and gradually became more comfortable. I found thoughts bubbling up to the surface. Yet there I was, years into the experience, and I was still reluctant to talk, fearing I could never ease their burden or, worse yet, I might say the wrong thing.

About three months later, I felt a shift. I'll never forget when a mother approached me and said, "I just don't know what to do anymore. My son won't stay on his medication. He takes it for a while, and as soon as he feels better, he goes off it, mainly because of the side effects. Then, all his symptoms return. His behavior becomes erratic. He gets agitated, then withdrawn. It's just a vicious cycle."

I nodded and began speaking. I shared what I had heard my husband say many times: that she wasn't alone. I shared that another mother found a certain group helpful in addressing the issue with meds. I shared that it gets easier with time. After she thanked me and I walked away, I realized that I had completely forgotten to be so reluctant. For the first time, I felt like I knew what to say. And from that moment on, I found I no longer had any hesitation about discussing schizophrenia.

A decade later, I got a call from a close family friend, Mary Ann, her voice barely a whisper. I could tell right away that she was terrified as she described her son's recent odd behavior. "Susan, we don't know what to do; Gary is acting so strange," she confided. As she continued to describe her situation, I suspected the worst. My heart sank. It was one thing to talk to strangers; it was another thing speaking with a dear friend whose son was having what turned out to be a psychotic episode. Watching it happen to someone with whom I was close, I couldn't help thinking, *What if this were my child? Our lives would be altered forever.* Schizophrenia became real to me in a new way.

"If only Mary Ann could talk about Gary's condition with other people," I said to Sam. "If he had any other illness, her friends would be rallying around and offering their support by taking over food, visiting, and acknowledging what's happening in the family."

※

Two years ago, I had a conversation that underscored just how far I'd come. I was standing by the lockers at an upscale spa. An attractive woman close to my age, grabbing her bathing suit, asked if I lived in San Diego.

"Yes, I do live part-time in San Diego," I said.

She nodded, smiled, feeling some sense of kinship. She too lived in San Diego part-time and shared, "Our place is on Coronado. How about yours?"

"Oh, we live across from Balboa Park."

Her face scrunched up in distaste. "Why would you want to live there? There are so many homeless people in the park."

Without missing a beat, I replied, "Many of the homeless are mentally ill, and I'm sympathetic to their situation."

And then suddenly, her façade cracked. She looked me in the eyes, and I saw the pain I'd seen many times in the eyes of so many family members.

"You know, my brother is homeless. He was diagnosed with schizophrenia and lives in Albuquerque."

As I drove home that night, I thought back on our life. Here it was, forty years later, and people were still reluctant to talk about schizophrenia. My mind went immediately back to that question I was asked right before we were married.

"Why would anyone be interested in working with people with schizophrenia?" I pulled into the driveway proud, grateful, and perplexed all at once. Proud that Sam had dedicated his professional career to improving diagnosis and treatment and to helping communities understand the illness. Proud that I had been a small part of it all. Grateful for the journey, for how profoundly I'd been changed. And yet perplexed. What was it going to take to get this country to start this essential conversation?

HE JUMPED BUT I FELL

CAROLINE GILMAN

Starbucks, Los Angeles, 2007.

I was twenty-seven, late for work and watching a conveyor belt of robots coming and going out the revolving door, carrying their white paper cups with the green logo. I was in line, sleepwalking through my morning, head in my phone. Trying not to be noticed. Or to notice anyone. Then the inevitable happened when the lady in front of me—decked out from head to toe in Lululemon as if working out was her sole occupation—placed her order.

"I'll have a grande iced sugar-free latte with soy milk, four pumps of caramel and half a pump of vanilla, easy on the ice."

I sighed. She continued.

"Actually, make it a venti, please, and can I have double whip and some chocolate drizzle?" The barista managed to keep her smile as she tossed the grande cup and started over with a venti.

I normally take my coffee and run, but this day was different. I was excited to meet my ex-boyfriend Marcus after a long absence. He was a disciplined, hard-working marine that I hadn't seen in over a year. I had emailed him about a dream I had, and he responded quickly, saying he had experienced the same dream and wanted to meet.

It didn't matter what Marcus's title was in my life—boyfriend, ex-boyfriend, or friend. We often had a synchronistic relationship and knew what the other was feeling or thinking, even without speaking for months at a time.

When he walked in, I looked up timidly, holding back my inner excitement, and waved. I was taken back by his thin frame and hunched shoulders. He looked frail. *Had I remembered him as larger than he actually was? Taller? More robust and marine-like?* It felt like when you revisit your childhood home and realize how much smaller your room looks. I hugged him. No, it wasn't just my imagination; he was much, much thinner. And his self-assured presence—it wasn't there.

We sat for a moment. He offered a half-smile and then started frantically scanning the room, his eyes bouncing from the front door to the bathroom and back again. I asked how he was, but he didn't answer; he only continued to look around nervously.

"Everything okay?" I tried again. He shook his head as if trying to shake off a layer of anxiety, nodded yes, and then in the same breath grabbed my hand and took off for the exit. He dragged me like a rag doll through the Starbucks and out the door. He found a table outside, and we sat down. He was fidgeting in his seat with sweat pooling on his forehead. It wasn't hot out at all.

"How are you?"

"I broke up with her. She made you look like a neat freak," he said.

"Your girlfriend?" I asked. He nodded. I knew that he was not complimenting my neatness, but rather insulting his girlfriend, as I had never met the marine guidelines for organization or tidiness.

"Plus, she was mean to me." He paused. "Yesterday she threw a glass bottle at my head. So, I left."

I could see the pain in his eyes, and I could feel his cavernous sadness in the pit of my stomach.

Where was my friend, the veteran who conducted himself with strength, order, and discipline? How had he become okay with living in chaos? Why was he so skinny and sweating?

Before I had time to ask any questions, he scanned the cars parked in front of us, his eyes darting from row to row like he was part of a security team searching for a bad guy.

"I gotta get out of here; I can't stay."

"Do you want to grab some food first? You look like you could eat."

He gave me a harsh glare and then looked away.

"No, I gotta go."

In confusion, I hugged Marcus, and he left, leaving me with more questions than answers.

A few weeks later, I walked out of the same Starbucks, cup in hand, when I got the call. The kind of call that separates your life into before and after. I answered, surprised to hear Marcus's brother on the other line. I turned to lean on my car as we spoke.

"He's gone," he said.

"What?"

"He's gone," he kept saying. "He's gone."

Logical me was racking my brain, trying to think of where Marcus might be hiding out.

Perhaps he went down to the meditation gardens to clear his head. Or maybe he went to visit his daughter, or a drive alone to think.

Then his brother's voice broke through the noise in my head.

"No, you aren't understanding, he's gone, there was an accident."

"An accident? Is he okay?"

"He's dead, Caroline. He jumped from a freeway overpass onto the road below. He's dead, man, he's gone."

The words pierced my soul. I slid from the car down to the ground. I felt myself shrieking, but no audible sound came out of my mouth. My body stopped functioning. My heart was in my throat, and I was choking on it while lying on the freshly repaved Starbucks parking lot, bright-white newly painted parking-stall stripes and all.

I am not sure how much time passed before I finally realized that my brain had to tell my body to breathe. It was like someone unmuted me, and I could hear myself crying. And then, I actually felt myself leave my own body—and slowly—I rose above it all. I could see myself crying on the pavement, yet I was also aware of the action all around me. People were passing me by, life as normal, going in, and then coming out with their green-logo'd cups. Some ignored me completely; others looked at me and paused for a moment before continuing on their way.

To this day, I associate Starbucks, not with the smell of freshly brewed coffee, but rather the smell of asphalt. Salty, hot, bitter-smelling asphalt.

Marcus jumped that day, but I fell. In fact, I broke.

I was left with only wide, gaping questions. Questions that nobody can answer. Why didn't he call me if he was struggling? What happens to someone after death? He had been my spiritual mentor for so many years, and now I was left questioning what happens to someone who ends their own life. How did I not recognize that he was deep into drugs? Was he now at peace? And why, if he was at peace, am I the one left here in this hell, missing him?

A broken mess of questions and unending sadness: that's what I became after that phone call. And while it took years to work through the pain, I found it was the pain itself that was slowly transforming me—waking me up. Somehow, sleepwalking through life no longer seemed an option. Life for me had become violently precious. I found I was walking with intention; my eyes felt more open, and my love felt more ready.

Twelve years have passed, and now when I walk into a Starbucks, I no longer see a line of robots. I don't even notice the white cups in their hands or roll my eyes at difficult orders. Instead, I see the man behind that cup grieving a sick and dying father; a single mother behind her cup wondering how she will pay the rent; and a child who is silently suffering from bullying in school. And often, I won't just walk by. I stop, put down my green-logo'd cup and offer a shoulder to cry on, a hug, or an ear to listen because I know the silent demons that we all carry and don't talk about, but should.

WHAT NOT TO SAY IN AN ARRANGED MARRIAGE

SAADIA ALI ESMAIL

I was twenty-five; the clock was ticking. LOUD. In my culture, I was already an old maid. All of my cousins had been married straight out of college.

My parents' pressure came in an unspoken way. Except when they tossed off casual comments like, "Oh, did you hear Insia got married; and she's only twenty-four!"

And then there was the day that my mother's friend came over for tea. I was upstairs when I overheard, "Any proposals for Saadia yet?"

Mom hesitated, then spoke with a bit of shame in her voice.

"No, but God willing, soon."

My cheeks flushed. I was awash in a mix of embarrassment for my mom and rage for myself. It was clear. The eyes of the community were on her.

I grew up in Long Island, New York. My parents were first-generation from Pakistan. We belonged to the sect of Islam called Dawoodi Bohras, an offshoot of Shi'ism. We followed the traditions that have been going on for hundreds of years. Male matches were judged on their background, reputation, and profession. Women faced different judgments: What's her personality? How tall is she, is she pretty, is she healthy?

And then, there was me. Twenty-five years old with an autoimmune disease no one had heard of called Myasthenia Gravis

(MG). It's a chronic disease with no cure. It meant that one day I could talk; but the next day, I couldn't. One day, I could walk; the next day, I couldn't.

I had always wanted to be a wife. But I was looking for my best friend. I wanted something different from my parents. My father was the dominating force in their relationship, and I often felt my mom deserved to be treated with more respect. I wanted the laughter and the humor that I all too often did not see.

I had received proposals, met them in person, but nothing was clicking.

On a trip to Pakistan, my aunt mentioned someone new—his name was Ali. His mother and his aunt came to my aunt's home. They talked; I listened. After they left, my aunt showed me Ali's picture. Decent, I thought.

When I returned home, his cousin called my mom, asking if she could bring Ali over.

Our first meeting was for lunch. It was a wintry, snowy day. When my mom told me he was coming, I was less than excited. I had plans to go car shopping. And I had just overcome an MG crisis; due to steroids, my face was bloated, and I had acne everywhere. I was sure he would take one look at me and run the other way.

When he came to the door, I was so nervous I couldn't face him yet. He spoke to my parents for a half hour. I could hear chuckles and laughter. When they moved into the family room, I knew I had to gather my strength and meet him.

And our eyes met. Me: a shy bundle of nerves. Him: a tall, respectable young man. And all eyes were on us. It was a formal meeting. But I was happy when he asked for my email address, and we began corresponding.

We talked hopes, careers, hobbies.

He loved playing the piano. I did too.

He loved hiking and exploring nature. I did too.

He cracked jokes. He made me laugh—this was the beginning of a real connection.

We wrote two or three emails a day—and with each email, we grew closer. And my heart grew more invested.

And then came the moment to tell him of my disease.

I was terrified. Would he run? I decided to tell him over email. I remember hitting send with my fingers trembling, feeling stripped bare.

I was so relieved when he wanted to meet again, coming to my home with an open heart and a box of Russell Stover chocolates. He asked MG-related questions as if it was a minor scrape, not a chronic illness.

I knew I wanted to marry Ali when we went out together. We were in the car, and he shifted in his seat and said, "Where do we go from here?"

"I am taking the highway, and we will see the monuments."

"No, Saadia, where do *we* go from here?" he repeated.

At the time, I felt that Ali was my savior, my ticket to freedom. Contrary to the path my parents took, with Ali, I could do what I wanted. I could break free from my overprotective parents and live out the dreams that were mine and mine only.

I had always thought "love at first sight" was just a cliché. But here I was living it. I loved the terms of endearment that Ali had already started calling me, my favorite being Bibi, a respectful way to address a lady in Urdu. Countless other things, trivial and otherwise that had unknowingly, unexpectedly, joined our hearts together.

But there was a hurdle. Both our parents had to agree. Mine were thrilled. I hoped his would be too.

A week later, I got a call from Ali. I could hear the strain in his voice.

"Mom didn't take it as well as I thought she would. She said no."

I was awash in emotions. We had agreed not to tell anyone about my MG before we became officially engaged.

"What did you expect, Ali?" I wanted to remain calm, but I could control neither my sarcasm nor my anger, anger at Ali for telling his mother about my disease, and anger at her for not understanding. I felt out of control—like a puppet, my strings being pulled at the whim of the puppeteer.

Her resistance confirmed my secret doubts: I was damaged goods.

"Honestly, I wish I didn't tell her anything, Saadia."

"Her son wants to marry someone with a disease she's never even heard of. Of course, she's going to panic and say no!"

I was certain he could hear my heart hammering through the phone line. It jarred the silence like a referee's whistle signaling an unexpected timeout, or in my case, the end of the game. *If this didn't work, if his mother rejected me, would I ever get married?*

"She's asked for some time."

"How much time?"

A deep breath. I wasn't sure if it was his or mine.

"A few days, I guess."

I slouched on the edge of my bed.

"Saadia, this is our culture. We marry into a family, and family cannot be ignored."

There it was again, our culture. Why couldn't we ignore what our families thought?

As it often did, it all came back down to respect. Respect your elders; don't go against their wishes.

"Give her some time."

My stomach dropped. Had I lost Ali already?

"She knows that I have my heart set on you."

"And what if you can't convince her?"

"Then you can cross me off your list and pick the next guy."

"That's not funny, Ali," I shot back.

I knew he was trying to calm me down. And that's what I liked about him the most.

"I'm sorry, Saadia. But I promise we'll be stronger for it."

A day passed. Then two. Then three.

On day four, I found myself trudging around the house when an idea began to form. What if I wrote to his mother—shared with her from my heart? This was not done in our culture. Not. Ever. Done.

Could I be so bold, did I dare? And what if it backfired?

But here was a man who I was beginning to love, someone who I could envision spending my life with. I had to try at least. So, I opened up my email and started writing. I didn't want her to think my life revolved around the disease, because it didn't. I was able to work, to finish my Master's even when the disease was at its worst. I was able to exercise and swim, to cook and do the laundry. I was able to socialize, to talk and laugh.

I told her there was a good chance that the MG would go into remission. I did not tell her that, on average, it could take up to five years for remission to occur and, even then, it was not guaranteed.

I told her that having this disease, in spite of its drawbacks and repercussions, had made me a stronger person. I did not tell her how many nights I cried in prayer and in sleep when no one could understand me because my mouth would not let out any words.

As scared as I was, it felt liberating to be free of the secret—or at least part of my secret. I had lowered my mask just enough to let her in. It may not have been the full truth, but it was more daring than any girl in my culture would have dreamed. Calmness spread from the top of my head to the tips of my toes. Whatever she decided, I knew in my heart that I would fight for Ali and he for me. My hands felt clammy.

I took in a deep breath, exhaled a prayer, and pressed "Send."

YOU SHOULD SAY GOODBYE

MARDESTINEE C. PEREZ

"You should say goodbye to him before you leave," the home nurse said. I stood frozen in the doorway of my stepfather's room. For weeks I had passed his room every day without a single word. I couldn't bear to look at him. I knew if I saw how he lay motionless, connected to tubes and an oxygen tank, I would lose my resolve and soften. But something about the way she said it made me step inside.

It was June 1, 1998; I was fourteen years old, and in my first year of high school. My stepfather had been in a coma for a month and was now a skeleton of the man he had been before cancer. I stared at him with mixed emotions.

"What should I say?"

"Anything. Just let him know you're here."

"Hello, Father, it's Mar ... I'm going to school now ... Goodbye."

Quickly and without taking another look, I left. My stepfather had raised me since I was a baby and what I learned as I grew was this man I loved had two distinct faces. Most people knew him as compassionate, religious, and hardworking. He was a carpenter who worked tirelessly. I still get nostalgic at the smell of sawdust, which covered every inch of our back patio. I don't recall him ever complaining, even when he came home covered in dirt and sweat or hadn't eaten all day. We went to church on Wednesdays, Thursdays, occasionally on Fridays, and twice on Sundays. We sat in the very back so that Father could greet people as they entered the congregation. He always had his *güiro*, his *tambora*, and a collection of other Puerto Rican instruments he used to praise the Lord. The louder, the better.

During the blind innocence of childhood, I saw only kindness in my father. When I had an asthma attack, he stayed up with me or took me to urgent care. I adored his hands, weathered and calloused, the evidence of his life's work. Those rough hands were never too tired to hold me or stroke my hair so I could fall asleep. When he finally rested in the late evening to watch the nightly news and snack on salami, I'd snuggle up with him on his old brown recliner and sneak a few bites from his plate.

"Mar, let your father eat," my mom would say to me.

"You go ahead, *mi prieta chula*, eat whatever you want," he'd whisper. I was certain he'd give me his only water if we were ever stranded in a desert.

And yet, the man who was tender and kind to me was cold and cruel with the rest of my family. My sister's nickname for him was "the devil," in stark contrast to the godly man he wanted to be. He made a spanking paddle out of wood. Anytime my brother was out of line, my father would grab that paddle or take off his leather belt and shout, "Just keep it up, boy, and you'll see what'll happen." He called it discipline, but it never felt that way. His insults were biting and constant. Idiot. Imbecile. Fat. Lazy. When he was enraged, we often didn't know what he might do. Sometimes an argument ended with a broken coffee table or a hole punched through the door. Occasionally, Mom would take us and we would flee, but we always returned home.

Throughout the violence and drama, I was protected. If my father ever heard my mother raising her voice at me for any reason, he'd intervene. If my brother or sister picked on me or told me to shut up, he'd quickly retort. This special treatment made me feel both safe and uncomfortable. I did nothing to deserve the attention, and it seemed unfair that only I should be immune to his ugliness. And yet, I loved him for it. The more I understood, the worse I felt for accepting love from a man who was so destructive.

One evening, we were gathered at a church member's home. The kids were spread out on the floor, and a small group of us girls were talking. My older brother was being obnoxious and bothering us. We asked him to stop several times, until my father, overhearing the commotion, had enough. In front of our church friends, eyes enraged, he grabbed my brother by the arm, dragged him out of the house, and threw him down a flight of stairs. He fumed at us to get in the car, and we went home without another word.

Up until that evening, I had tried to justify my father's behavior. I believed he was a good man who just sometimes lost his temper. But when I saw the look of horror on everyone's faces and the fear in my brother's eyes as he was being thrown down the stairs, I thought, *How could I possibly love this monster?*

As my older siblings grew more rebellious, our father only became more aggressive. Yet after that night with the stairs, I felt responsible for protecting my siblings. When my father threatened my brother with a kitchen knife, I stepped in front of him, knowing Father would never hurt me. But no matter how hard I tried, I couldn't change him. Feeling powerless, I started calling him by his first name—Pedro—a rejection that hurt him as much as it pained me.

During that turbulent period, my father was diagnosed with lung cancer. All those years working in construction with asbestos caught up with him and his health quickly disintegrated. For the first time in my life, he seemed old and weak, no longer impervious to pain. As angry as I was, I wanted to hold his wrinkled face and give him the comfort he had given me when I was ill.

But I couldn't, even when his death was at our doorstep.

Expressing love for my father felt like a betrayal to my siblings. But not caring for the man who had always cared for me didn't feel right either. I'd always been taught to do the right thing, follow what Jesus would do. But even now, I don't know that there was a *right* choice. There was no justice in any of this, and yet my guilt weighed heavily. While my father suffered alone, I carried my emotions in silence and avoided feeling by trying to shut everyone out. I secretly held the small hope that on his deathbed, he would shock us all and seek atonement. Then I could forgive everything and openly care for him. In that dream, I'd beg him to ask my siblings for forgiveness and make things right before he left this earth. But he remained unrepentant.

The day I said goodbye, I was certain my father couldn't hear me, so I didn't give my words much thought. But sometime after noon, I got called to the principal's office.

"You're going home," he said, "your father died. I'm so sorry."

When I arrived home, my siblings were already there and visibly happy. I understood that for them, this meant freedom from a person that caused them so much harm. But their reaction made me feel sick, not only because I was heartbroken, but because the shameful truth was, I too was relieved that it was finally over.

I went to the backyard where no one would bother me, and I cried for hours. I felt my whole body shaking, trying to release the anger and sadness I'd been trying to suppress for years. When I couldn't possibly cry any more, I went back inside.

Today marks the twentieth anniversary of my father's death, and we still don't talk about him in my family. It's as if he never existed. Every now and then, when his name comes up, I'm overwhelmed by the memory of him emaciated, struggling to breathe. I wasn't able to openly grieve his passing twenty years ago and am only now making sense of my experience. The man who raised me was flawed. And yet, he showed me a generosity that was infinite and unconditional. I loved the man he wanted to be just as much as the imperfect man he wanted to hide.

As a child who believed in righteousness, I saw my loving heart as a weakness. For years after his passing, I tried to be tough, unfeeling. I now know that my father had a hard life, and I believe he acted out of his own unhealed trauma. That doesn't justify his behavior, but I recognize his pain and that he did the best he could. I regret withholding kindness from my father during his last days. I wish I'd done more to ease his suffering. I wish I'd given myself permission to say the words,

I forgive you, Father.

Will you forgive me?

SEX, SINS & SAWDUST

JOHN CUNNINGHAM

"Motherfucker, have you lost your mind? Do you know what my family would do to you?"

I was raised on a carnival, traveling with my family on the Royal American Shows, "the Show" for short, once considered the world's largest carnival midway. Momma and I traveled throughout the breadbasket of America and Canada in railroad sleeper cars; ours was Car #66. My aunt and uncle, Gwen and Leon Claxton, produced and performed in an all-black Las Vegas-style musical revue known as Harlem in Havana, one of the Show's main attractions.

It was the summer of 1958, I was seventeen years old, and though Momma and I hadn't traveled with the Show for over ten years, my Aunt Gwen and Uncle Leon had let me join them during the summer to earn money for school. I had met the Show in Winnipeg and planned to travel with them across Canada and several US cities before returning to Los Angeles and home.

We had pulled into Calgary early, and after the big top was set up, Momma's old boyfriend Dave and I stocked the pop stand with Orange Nehi, Royal Crown Cola, and Vernon's Ginger Ale. When we were done, we joined the tent hands spreading sawdust inside the big top.

Harlem's tent could seat over one thousand people plus the stage and dressing wagon areas, so it took a lot of sawdust. Though the fairground wasn't scheduled to open until the next morning, some of the midway's food joints were already up and running. The midway always had a distinct odor, a mixture of cotton candy, grilled onions and burgers, fresh sawdust, and the ever-present dank smell of old canvas. I grabbed a couple of burgers for dinner and headed back to the Show's cars. Dave and most of the other Show folks had already gone to town to stay in hotel rooms.

The train's old Pullman cars were built around 1928 and had never been updated. The dark gray painted bathroom opened to a large area that was curtained off into several bathing stalls where we used large galvanized steel laundry tubs and submersible electrical heater coils to warm the water. Two toilet stalls reminded me of outhouses; they smelled like them too.

Thinking the sleeper car was empty, I fixed myself a tub of water in the washroom and was washing my hair when one of the male dancers, who was new to me, came in and went into one of the stalls. I ignored him and continued to wash my hair when suddenly I felt hands fondling my balls. I almost fell over backward. I quickly opened my eyes, soap and all, to find the dancer kneeling in front of me with this goofy look.

Fear flashed through my body at first, but it instantly changed to anger, and I went into survivor mode. Coming down hard with both hands, hitting him squarely on top of his head, he fell backward on his butt. "Motherfucker, have you lost your mind? Do you know what my family would do to you?" Those were magic words; it appeared to strike pure fear in him. There was a strong smell of booze on his breath, and a small stream of blood trickled from his nose. Suddenly, remembering where *he* was and who *I* was, the dancer panicked and started stuttering as he apologized, crawling backward and stumbling to get to his feet.

I didn't tell anyone about the incident for fear that Dave, Uncle Leon, or anyone of the tent hands would have beat him within an inch of his sorry ass. The blow to his head had taken its toll; I was a big teenager, weighing at least 175 pounds. No one had dared mess with me in the past, so I'd never thought to worry. We were all family, or so I thought, but from that night on, I made damn sure someone else was around when I took my baths. For the rest of the summer, the dancer was a ghost.

We were on our way to our next stop, Edmonton, Alberta. I was feeling a little anxious about what had happened in the bathroom in Calgary and found myself distrusting those people I didn't know from the old days.

We stopped a few miles just outside of Edmonton and pulled on to a siding to allow a freight train to pass. While we were stopped, people got off to stretch. I noticed several members of the band walking over by a big water tank near the tracks. They were pulling what appeared to be weeds, stuffing them into pillowcases. Later, I found out the plants were just that—wild marijuana. Stopping at this particular siding was routine, so they tossed their marijuana seeds near the water tank and retrieved them the following year.

Setup in Edmonton went smoothly; we were done before dark, and the gates wouldn't open until noon the next day. Everyone looked forward to playing Canada, particularly Edmonton, because unlike at some US stops, we weren't called racial slurs or jeered there. Canadians truly welcomed us. Many first-time fairgoers had never seen a black person. I remember shopping downtown with Aunt Gwen and this little kid, standing next to us, was staring. He finally couldn't help himself and reached out and touched my skin and then looked at his hand. I thought his mother was going to die with embarrassment.

The next morning, I was up early and went out to the lot before most were up. I checked the pop stand to see what I needed to stock up on and was on my way to the supply wagon that was located out behind Harlem's huge tent. As I reached the back of the stage, I heard a girl's muffled voice cry out, "Let me go, please, let me go."

It was coming from under the stage where the tent hands had their bedrolls. Because of the tent's thick, heavy canvas, it was pitch-black under there, but, as my eyes adjusted, I could make out at least two people. Without thinking, I jumped down beside one of the dressing wagons and worked my way to the sounds. I saw Al, one of Harlem's musicians, and a young white girl that appeared to be in her early- to mid-twenties. He had one hand in her pants and the other holding her arm behind her back.

Seeing me, she pleaded even louder. "Hey, what the fuck are you doing, let her go!" I yelled. I could see now and realized that I had stumbled into a rape in progress. And, there was another couple under there. It was Young Blood, one of the tent hands, with another white girl; this one was much older, and she appeared to be enjoying herself. She and Young Blood were going at it, oblivious to anyone around them. I heard Al say, "Shut up, bitch."

I was sweating, and my heart was racing. *What the fuck?* I thought, yelling at him again to let her go.

He laughingly said, "This ain't none of your business, kid; you just go on back out front now."

I never liked that son of a bitch. I could see the fear in the girl's eyes as she pleaded, "Please make him let me go." Hearing what was going on, the other two got up and pulled on their clothes.

Al turned toward me and more forcefully said, "I told you this ain't none of your business; now beat it!"

I took a deep breath as a rush of adrenaline went through me, and I said, "Let her go now, Al, or I will tell my uncle."

You would have thought I shoved a hot poker up his ass. "Ah shit, kid, don't use my name." With that, he pulled his hand out of her pants. As he did, I reached down and grabbed the girl's hand, pulling her up and away. The other couple had already moved out from under the stage, and Young Blood had a panicked look on his face as I rushed both girls toward an opening in the tent's sidewall, shoving them outside. I could see both fear and thanks on the girl's tear-stained face.

Later that evening, Young Blood asked if we were cool. "You didn't do anything wrong, but your buddy Al better stay away from me." Once again, I didn't tell anyone, fearing they would have severally punished Al, who was in his fifties, and chastised Young Blood, twenty-three, whose only crime was associating with Al.

As I look back on that summer and those dark incidents, I wonder how many other young girls this had happened to; would my speaking up have changed anything? Ten years later, upon the death of my Uncle Leon, I received a letter from Momma telling me that he had raped her when she was seventeen and that Leon was my father. Her sister, Aunt Gwen, had begged her not to tell anyone until after he was gone, to protect his image and the Claxton family name.

What about my family's name? Cunningham was a shame, a name that was given to me to hide a dark secret. What would have happened had Momma spoken up and given me her maiden name, or better yet, the Claxton name? I think her whole family knew and never talked about it. As for the Claxton dynasty, well, we don't talk about it either; it no longer exists.

THAT WHICH SHALL BE NAMED

LAURA JAYE

Sunlight poured over my left shoulder as I sat, cross-legged on the floor, gazing up at my father. He sat in a wheelchair, wearing a white Hanes T-shirt and blue shorts, just like the ones I had seen him wear so many times as a child. He had lost the use of his left arm and leg because of the brain tumor; his exposed legs were swollen; his skin bruised, fragile, and paper-thin; his voice impaired. But his gaze was direct and, though I knew he physically could not hurt me, at the age of thirty-one, I still felt a familiar sense of unease being alone in the room with him.

"Laura, when you were a kid," my father began, taking the time to articulate each word deliberately, "you were raped by a babysitter. There were signs that it had happened, and I am sorry that I never did anything about it. I didn't go to the police, and I didn't take you to therapy." Tears rose to my eyes. I was shocked to see his mouth form the words that finally confirmed a truth that I had internally known.

A hurricane of memories hurled toward me. All throughout my teenage years, I had questioned my parents repeatedly, "Did something happen to me as a kid?"

Their response was always "No."

Yet I had this weird creepy-crawly feeling that there was something under the surface that I couldn't remember. I felt a crazy-making panic because their reality never matched mine. I thought, *I must be nuts.*

Nothing had made sense. Why, as a young teenager, was I terrified to look and dress like a girl? I was bulimic by at the age of fourteen, attempting to control the changes in my body. Self-hatred penetrated my entire being. The anger that I felt inside threatened to explode, like the nightmares I had about a bomb in my dresser, ticking away.

Instead, I imploded. I resorted to picking the scabs on my skin, never letting them heal. I hid in the bathroom regularly to pierce my ears by hand. When boys became interested in me, I averted their attention and avoided them out of primordial fear. A fear that had no name or explanation.

I remembered a moment when I was sixteen and was enraged by my parents. There I was, sitting on the small, grassy but manicured hill next to our driveway, cigarette in between my fingers. My dad lumbered out of the garage and climbed up the hill. He stopped, put his hands in his pockets, and looked at me nervously. Smoking the cigarette on the hill was the last bit of rebellion I had in me, and I simply didn't care what anyone thought anymore. In that moment, I felt screwed living in that house—and hopeless because I couldn't leave, no matter how many times I tried. He just stood there with me, without words.

The next year, at seventeen, I had a failed suicide attempt that landed me in a psych ward for teens. Afterward, I started partying with friends and drank like an alcoholic from the get-go. The first time I got drunk, I was so out of control that I kissed five guys and proceeded to throw up until four in the morning. My only thought afterward was *I want to do it again.* It numbed the hurt. It freed me from inhibition. It made me feel happy, like I was okay.

However, by the age of twenty-one, drinking took me to an emotional space where I could no longer control the desire to kill myself. It was stop drinking or die. I had a choice to make as I sat there in the water-filled bathtub, staring at my reflection in metal drain lever, with a razor in my hand. I chose to get sober.

Within weeks of this decision, I started experiencing a repetitive physical sensation of being raped that made no sense, since, to my knowledge, I'd never had sex. The dark memories tormented me as I tried to hide under the covers, alone in my bed, crying hysterically.

I slowly started to heal and at the age of twenty-three, I finally had the courage to own the truth with my family. I directly asked my parents at the bagel shop where we went to eat, "What happened to me? I know I was raped; I have the physical memories, but I can't remember who it was."

"I don't know anything," my mom said in a sugary voice from across the table. My heart fell in frustration; I couldn't get past her brick wall. Denial, her standard response. I looked at my dad. He had his head in his right hand and stated softly, "I should never have let that happen." His acknowledgment of something was so unexpected; I froze in confusion. I didn't understand his words, but I couldn't even think to ask for clarification. All I could do was stammer, "It's okay, Dad, you didn't know." We stopped talking and left the restaurant. The door closed behind us; we never talked about it again.

When I was twenty-five, my mind finally revealed the rapist's face backlit by the hall light outside of my childhood bedroom. He had dark curly hair. He was the boyfriend of our new blond babysitter.

Four years later, the rest of it surfaced. I reexperienced, in full emotional and bodily detail, what he had done to me in the living room on the Persian carpet, while she watched. I was six years old.

At that point, I didn't know if I would ever heal. I lay on my apartment floor in the fetal position, crying as I remembered my arms bound in front of me with my right cheek pressed against the carpet. I saw his sweaty face and left arm as he leaned over and leered at me with a salty grin. Then my mind left my body. I remember nothing until I recall a hazy visual of the '70s green carpet under the wooden toybox in the living room, along with a shameful realization that I had lost control of my bladder. My cold body shook in shock, and everything went dark.

Back at the nursing home, the sun was still shining, but my world was starting to fall apart with my dad's disclosure of a painful truth. He was watching me, waiting for me to mentally return to the room. When I focused my eyes on him, he continued. He had an intense look on his face that told me there was something he felt he needed to say.

"When you were four, you crawled onto my lap, and I had an erection—"

At that point, the dam burst. I started bawling. He stopped. He sat there in his wheelchair and watched me as I wrapped my arms around my knees and sobbed into my arms.

Something incredible occurred in that moment. Two memories, which I never understood, connected. One: the father-daughter dance when I was eight, and I refused to take a photo with my father at crotch level. Instead, I stood on a stool next to him, in a frilly pink dress that I detested, and put my arm around his shoulder. The result—an odd picture of a very tiny person trying to put her arm around an adult's shoulder. I remember facing him while dancing, only for a few seconds, before saying, "I need to go to the bathroom," then quickly walking away, but a part of me staying frozen in the spot, numb, watching myself hurry away.

Next: my dad stood outside the laundry room in a matching outfit to the one he was wearing that day in the nursing home. The sun had filled the room from the left on that morning too. I remembered him holding up his white cotton briefs to his crotch and asking me, "What do you think of these, Laura?" I was ten. Bile again. There was always bile. I said nothing and walked away quickly. I always, always wanted to get away.

In the nursing home with my father, my heart shook inside of my ribcage. I simultaneously felt so much pain from the truth itself, but then a newfound awareness emerged: *I am not crazy. It all makes sense.* I felt a little bit of hope grow as I saw for the first time that I could trust my memories.

I looked up at Dad. His face was tired with exhaustion as he tried to hold himself up in the wheelchair. I saw how weak he was and felt a moment of sadness. The nurse came in to help move him back to his bed. The bed from which he would pass to the other side.

I gently sat down next to him. This time the sun was getting lower in the sky, and shadows started to reach across the room. As I looked at the shadows, I started crying again. He placed his hand on my shoulder. I turned toward him and laid my head on his chest. He held me as a real father should, for the first time.

SECRETS

MADONNA TREADWAY

It is the first week in our new place, and I am walking home from school to our new apartment. I am seven.

When my mom died, we moved away from our family home. And if that wasn't hard enough, now my dad's in the hospital.

Even though this is all happening to me, I am North Dakota fierce, all guts and long blond hair.

Our neighbor lady, who lives two doors down from us is in her yard. She smiles and says, "Hi." Her smile is like an open door inviting me in.

"Hi," I say, finding I am not the least bit shy with her. We talk like we are old friends, and she asks about school.

"I am in the second grade, and I go to St. Michael's School. My name is Madonna Rose, and I live with my three brothers and my pop. My two older brothers, Fred and Frank, are in college. Eugene is in high school.

"And your parents?" she asks.

"Well, my dad is in the hospital, and we are waiting for him to come home."

"What is your father's name?"

"Fredrick Rose."

Then, as if thinking aloud, she says, "Someone in our church by that name died recently."

I blink. The breath catches in my throat. A sense of panic is roaring around me, threatening to swallow me whole.

I blurt out, "I have to go home now!" and I run.

My head is reeling, and my thoughts are swirling as I run. Is it true? Not Daddy!

Yes.

In my heart, I know it is.

I arrive at our apartment to find my oldest brother standing in the kitchen. I am filled with indignation as I proclaim, "I know what happened; I know my daddy is dead."

I cannot remember what he said. I walked into my room and wondered, *why didn't anyone tell me?* My stomach felt like it was turning inside out, and my mind was racing. And then a wave of terror swelled up and consumed me. First, my mother died. Then, my father. They were there, holding me, cuddling me, I could crawl onto their laps and tuck myself into them—and then they just disappeared. I wondered what else my brothers were not telling me. I was so filled with fury. I wanted to yell as loud as I could at my brothers and push them away. But I also wanted to cling to them for dear life.

No one explained how he died.

How was I to know that I actually already knew?

A week or so back, I had found Daddy. Like every other day, I ran happily into the apartment after school to greet my dad and tell him about my day. But this time, instead of finding him waiting for me, arms outstretched, what I saw was just blood. Blood everywhere. Thick and red, on the cold hardwood floor and under the velvety couch.

My eyes dart across the couch to the leg of his khakis with a dark red stain. My father is slumped to one side, and I cannot see his face. I don't know what is wrong. My stomach starts to hurt, and I feel sick. I'm not sure what this means, and I want to cry. Then in a flash, the strong arms of my brother scoop me up. Protectively, he pulls me close, and he runs out of the apartment with me in his arms. He runs down the creaky stairs of the second-story apartment. He is so quiet, and I hold my breath.

What is happening?

As my brother drives, I am reeling with dread. I want to hug my dad and make it all better. I know my dad is already so sad. He had already lost the use of half of his body because of the stroke he had after my mama died. He could barely get words out. After school, he would call me over and try as hard as he could to speak to me. I saw the pain in his eyes as he tried to speak—"Douunna, Dowwwna," he would get out painfully as he reached for the right way to say, Donna. I think of this and want to cry again. I just can't right now. I swallow hard. My brother leaves me with a friend of the family, and he runs out of the house.

Somehow, that night, because of all the blood, I concluded that my father died of a heart attack. And no one told me any different.

I live in Fargo, North Dakota with my brother and his family. I'm a sophomore in high school. I'm at the public library—one of my favorite escapes.

I continued to believe that my father died of a heart attack until I was fourteen years old. I was reading a magazine article about what happens when a person has a heart attack, and there was no mention of blood.

Yet what I remembered was a lot of blood. This had me puzzled, and I began thinking about that day that I had pushed deep down into my memory. *What about all that blood? What did that mean?*

I went home and asked my sister-in-law what happened.

"What really happened to my father?"

She looked at me, stricken, in shock, but said nothing.

"Where did all that blood come from?" I asked.

Still, no answer. I was insistent. My sister-in-law called my brother, who was traveling, to talk to me. I cannot remember the conversation, yet it came out that my father had put a gun in his mouth.

A tornado of emotions flooded my body. I could not believe it, and yet it was true. I was suddenly seven all over again, looking at his body, the blood on his slacks and the couch. I could not hold back the wave of tears that poured. I yelled, I cried, I was betrayed. I was crushed. I was abandoned.

Then it passed, and we never talked about it again.

It became clear to me that it was a family secret. I learned that my grandmother was never told how her son had died.

And we never really talked about them—Mom or Dad. There were no lovingly framed photos of my parents in our home after their deaths. There was no recollection of pleasant memories around the kitchen table with them in the picture, although I understood my brothers loved them.

But still, I had no one to fill in the blanks about who my parents were as people or as parents. The only picture I had was the one that expanded in my imagination.

I simply wouldn't know what it would be like to have them at graduations, or at my wedding.

If a teacher asked me what my father did for a living, I would deflect, maybe ask about them. Anything to get the attention off of me. So, I put my head down, went to school, and got good grades. Moving on was what we did. Moving on was survival.

❦

I was forty when I started talking about it.

I began what would turn out to be life-changing therapy. Early on, my therapist asked what I thought about my parents having died so early in my young life.

I remember tossing off, "Oh, I've dealt with all that."

She explained that that was not the way it worked.

And indeed, she was right. It wasn't. Not talking about things, it turns out, doesn't make them invisible. One by one, day by day, the secrets made their way to the surface. Laid bare to be trekked through with tears and a well of grief so endless I thought I would never find my way out.

And then, relief.

And then, a recognition of my insane resilience.

So much so, that whenever I am stopped by something life throws at me, all I have to do is remember that seven-year-old I was, long blond hair, North Dakota accent, all guts.

RITE OF PASSAGE

MELISSA BLOOM

At thirteen, the world was divided into good and evil. I was part of the Harry Potter generation, and between Harry and Voldemort, I knew which side I was on. I was also part of the 9/11 generation, when terrorism became a household topic. In fantasy, when given a choice between good and evil, it is easy to choose the side of good. In reality, that decision is much more muddled.

When the last bell of seventh grade rang in June of 2002, I brushed my hands of adolescence and prepared for my Jewish rite of passage. My bat mitzvah would mark a new chapter. I would turn thirteen and leave my childhood behind.

Judaism had always been a part of my life because of my family upbringing, but even more so because of my cousin, Marla. Eleven years apart, we both had brown eyes and brown hair, mine frizzy and unruly at the onset of hormones, hers effortlessly wavy. She was poised and intelligent, but down-to-earth and fun-loving too. Whenever our extended family gathered, I made a beeline for Marla. I didn't remember choosing her as my role model. It was something I knew as sure as the sunrise.

No one was surprised when Marla was accepted at Hebrew University in Israel for graduate school. It was the world she fit so perfectly within.

At a family gathering before she left, I asked, "You're really going to Israel?"

"I'm going to study there so I can be a rabbi."

"Maybe I could be a rabbi someday?"

Marla's smile widened to reveal perfect, bright teeth. "You would make a great rabbi."

For me, Marla represented all the good that Judaism could be: the prayers, the songs, the community. I was in awe of her intelligence and bravery.

Everyone knew how dangerous it was in Israel. Thanks to 9/11 just a year before, I knew what terrorism was. But Marla wasn't afraid. She would have been in Gryffindor house if she went to Hogwarts.

Marla had been studying at Hebrew University for almost two years and was set to come home to visit two days before my bat mitzvah. There was no question she'd be coming, and I couldn't wait to show her all I had learned.

The day before her flight, I lounged with my sister on the couch, playing cards, trying to calm my nerves and excitement about my bat mitzvah. Both of us were oblivious to the telephone ringing and my mom's muffled, concerned voice from the other room.

Moments later, she stood before us and said, "They can't find Marla."

My mom turned on the news to images of rubble and ambulances and people running from a tan building. The caption below read: *Breaking News: Bombing at Hebrew University.*

She shook her head as she watched the chaos on the screen. "Marla and her friends have a meeting point for emergencies, but she never showed. She had one more exam."

One more exam.

My family gathered at my great aunt's sepia house, waiting hours for news about Marla. A pit grew in my stomach. The television flashed across the room, the same footage replaying. For the third time, I watched two men rushing a body on a gurney toward an ambulance. The body was on its side, head facing away from the camera. But this time, I noticed two things I hadn't noticed before: wavy brown hair and a dark red stain over the entirety of the victim's back.

My heart clenched. *It couldn't be.*

The phone rang. My great aunt fumbled with the receiver and held it to her ear. A collective breath sucked the air out of the room.

I waited for a smile to spread over her face, but instead, she dropped the phone as tears came out in an agonized wail.

And I realized I already knew. I knew as soon as I saw the TV footage of the body on the gurney. The wavy brown hair and dark red stain belonged to Marla.

Pressure built behind my eyes, confusion twisting in my gut. I needed someone to say it. To tell me that Marla wasn't getting on a plane. Wasn't coming home in two days. Wasn't attending my bat mitzvah. Wasn't ever coming back.

But no one did.

That night, masked men invaded my dreams. They stormed the temple with machine guns as I stood at the podium, reading from the Torah. I woke in a cold sweat.

"I can't do it," I said to my parents the next morning. "I want to cancel."

"Marla wouldn't want you to," they both said, and I knew they were right.

Not going through with my bat mitzvah went against everything Marla stood for and what she died for. But still, the fear gnawed at me as I walked through the temple doors the day of my bat mitzvah. I stared up at the high-domed ceiling, the blue-carpeted stairs leading to the stage, the carefully protected Torahs behind hand-crafted wooden cabinets. These symbols of my faith and culture were now a reminder that Marla was gone.

My family sat with me on the stage. The masked men crept into my mind, but I pushed them away. My body remained numb as I began to move through the motions of the ceremony.

A few minutes in, the large wooden door in the back of the room creaked open. Time moved in slow motion as Marla's parents and sister snuck into the back of the temple with dark sunglasses covering their faces.

But they had shown up. Because that's what Marla would have wanted—from all of us. To overcome the fear and carry on.

I took a deep breath and continued my Torah portion. Read my speech slowly and calmly. Recited the prayers that I knew like the back of my hand. As I read the words, it hit me: I didn't know what I was saying. I knew what to say, when to bow, when to stand on tiptoes, but this was the first moment I ever wondered, Why?

Until then, I had never questioned anything about my religion. Had never wondered if there could be a bad side. But regardless of how I felt, I knew everyone needed me to fight. And if I lost, then evil could win. The only problem was, it felt like evil already had.

Every prayer, every minute, was punctuated by Marla's absence. None of it should have required extra effort, and yet every word felt like hauling bricks across the yard. Somehow, I completed the ceremony. For Marla. For myself. For everyone who had shown up. To honor Judaism. To show that we would overcome, as our ancestors did, in the face of adversity. *But why didn't I feel anything other than numbness?*

Judaism, for me, had turned from a source of celebration, of community, and belonging, to a source of confusion, of what separates us, of how we are different.

After the ceremony and during the party, all I wanted was to go home and shut myself in my room. When I finally did, the confusion swelled in my head. I had been so concerned with checking all the items off the list—studying, memorizing, reciting the prayers perfectly.

And it meant nothing to me.

All I could think about was that Marla wasn't there. That I was scared. That I didn't know how I felt about any of it. That those words weren't worth my life. Or hers.

But for her, they were. And it took me years to recognize that that was where we were so different.

After Marla died, being Jewish no longer defined me. I didn't want to be an advocate like Marla. I didn't want to confront the people who killed my cousin. Or anyone who fought against the religious freedom of others. I just wanted to be a normal thirteen-year-old girl. I wanted to live despite my religion, not because of it.

Marla's death personified that the world is complex and not black and white. Talking openly about Marla is still hard because there are so many layers to what I believe and how I feel, twisted and blended through the years like a rainbow pack of modeling clay after many uses.

Marla's name and her story have carried on throughout the Jewish community as a symbol of hope and inspiration. They have written articles about her, included her in documentaries, opened buildings in her honor. But none of that changes what happened and how it happened. And none of that reconciles our major difference: that she was prepared to die for her religion, and I am not.

I spent most of my life convinced that Marla's death was not my trauma; that because I locked up the wound and decided Judaism no longer defined me, I would not be affected. But not talking about it, not confronting it and processing it, has made it the most influential event of my life. I allowed the trauma to become the compass guiding my decisions. Sharing my story of her story means it can be a part of me, a small step in closing the wound. My way to honor Marla. Not with buildings or documentaries or journalistic articles on her life, but with my words.

THE END

ABOUT THE EDITORS

MARNI FREEDMAN

Marni Freedman (BFA, LMFT) is a produced, published, and award-winning writer. After graduating an award-winning student from the USC School of Filmic Writing, Marni began her career with *Two Goldsteins on Acid*, which was produced for the stage in Los Angeles. She worked as a script doctor for top film companies and worked as a script agent for the Mary Sue Seymour Agency. One of her plays was made into a film, *Playing Mona Lisa*, and was produced by Disney. Her award-winning play, *A Jewish Joke*, appeared Off-Broadway in 2019. Her most recent play, *Roosevelt: Charge The Bear* debuted in New York in October of 2019.

Marni is the co-founder and Programming Director for The San Diego Writers Festival, she runs the San Diego Writers Network, is the programming director for the San Diego Memoir Writers Association, is editor of *Shaking the Tree: brazen. short. memoir.*, a yearly anthology published by MCM Publishing.

Marni is also a therapist for artists and writers. Her welcoming, easy-going nature and solid background are the underpinnings of what makes her such a popular writing coach across the country. Marni is unique because she has a tool for almost everything; she has a way of taking complicated information and translating it into easy-to-grasp, step-by-step information. Her character worksheets and plotting devices have been met with rave reviews. She teaches writing workshops for UCSD Extension, at conferences and retreats across the country, and runs the Memoir Certificate Program at San Diego Writers Ink.

Marni's most recent book, *Permission to Roar: For Female Thought Leaders Ready to Write*, won four awards and is an Amazon Bestseller. She also wrote *7 Essential Writing Tools: That Will Absolutely Make Your Writing Better (And Enliven the Soul)*, and is currently writing her third book, *Write to Magic*.

She lives with her wonderfully talkative husband and son, and their two cats, Dorothy J. Witten and The Beef, who don't like each other. Within her community she is often referred to as Glenda, the Good Witch of Writing. You can also find Marni at TheFeistyWriter.com, a writing hub to help writers find and believe in their authentic voice, and subscribe to her award-winning newsletter, filled with author tips and resources at MarniFreedman.com.

TRACY J. JONES

Tracy J. Jones is a professional content writer and editor, ghostwriter, and copy editor with more than 25 years of experience writing and editing for private clients, nonprofits, and corporations including time is an executive speechwriter for companies such as KPMG LLP, the New York Times, and Avon Products, Inc. Tracy is a content editor and a feature writer at thefeistywriter.com. She's a producer, head judge, writing coach, and co-director of the annual San Diego Memoir Showcase. Tracy is the co-editor of the award-winning anthology, *Shaking the Tree: brazen. short. memoir.* She's a writing coach for the SDWI Certificate in Memoir Writing, a founding board member of the San Diego Memoir Writers Association, a volunteer manager and programming support for the San Diego Writers Festival, and has been a featured writer/performer in So Say We All's V.A.M.P. showcase.

Tracy was the editor for Marni Freedman's *7 Essential Writing Tools: That Will Absolutely Make Your Writing Better (And Enliven Your Soul).* She also edited Freedman's award-winning and Amazon bestseller, *Permission to Roar: for Female Thought Leaders Ready to Writer their Book.* She's currently turning her screenplay, *Don't Call Me Kitty!*, into a YA novel and plans to publish her memoir, *Starting Over at Ground Zero in 2020.* For more information, email Tracy at tjjones1@gmail.com.

ARE YOU A MEMOIRIST?

The San Diego Memoir Writers Association is a community of writers committed to the art and craft of memoir writing. Our purpose is to create a community of inspired, informed, and nurtured memoirists. We host monthly member meetings with speakers who educate our writers on both the craft and business of memoir writing, present an annual Memoir Showcase where five-minute pieces are professionally performed on stage, and support the San Diego Writers Festival. Writers of all levels are welcome and encouraged to join us to help build their own writing tribe.

https://sandiegowritersfestival.com
http://sdmwa.org

Winner of the 13th Annual
National Indie Excellence Award for
an Anthology

Available at amazon.com, barnesandnoble.com,
and indiebound.org.

Shaking the Tree: brazen. short. memoir. (Volume 1)

The Memoir Showcase is proud to present a selection of our most compelling true stories, drawn from our annual content. These pivotal portraits speak to our diverse community and its willingness to share the most challenging, awe-inspiring moments that make up the human experience. From a life-changing moment with a Maasai warrior to a wild and unexpected coming-of-age tale in a carnival, *Shaking the Tree* reveals moments of courage, humor, and vulnerability. The stories within these pages are breathtaking.

You can't make this stuff up.

IN VOLUME 1:

Made in United States
North Haven, CT
01 January 2024

46771496R00125